Donated By
Richard & Barbara
Jenkins

Roycroft Collectibles

Newly Revised Edition

Roycroft Collectibles

Including collector items related to
Elbert Hubbard, founder of the
Roycroft Shops

Charles F. Hamilton

SPS Publications
Post Office Box 787 • Eustis, Florida 32727 • USA

Acknowledgments

I wish here to express my gratitude to my wife, Virginia (a former curator of the Elbert Hubbard Library-Museum) for her important help and suggestions; to the late Nancy Hubbard Brady for her encouragement; and to my son Grant Hamilton for his major photographic contributions to this work. My thanks, too, to son Charles B. Hamilton for valuable suggestions on the final draft of the manuscript, and for his extensive research of online auctions for this new edition. I also want to express my deep appreciation to editor Barbara A. Tieger for her assistance and counsel. Unless otherwise credited herein, the illustrations in this book are from the author's private collection.

Hamilton, Charles Franklin, 1915–
    Roycroft collectibles.
    Includes index
1. Roycroft Shop, East Aurora, N.Y.—Collectibles.
2. Hubbard, Elbert, 1856-1915—Collectibles.
3. Hubbard, Elbert, 1856-1915—Biography.
4. Authors, American—19th century—Biography.
5. Printers—United States—Biography. I. Title.

Library of Congress Catalog Card Number: 92-60083
ISBN 1-881099-25-3

Printed in the United States of America.

For more information on the Roycrofters or for details on related books, write to
SPS Publications • Post Office Box 787 • Eustis, Florida 32727• USA
Find us on the Web at roycroftbooks.com

Contents

Preface to the 2001 Edition

More than a century ago when Elbert Hubbard spoke of the now-treasured American Arts & Crafts era creations of his Roycroft Shops, he called them "things Roycroftie." He couldn't then have imagined the future significance of the *"e"* in "Roycroftie." And twenty-one years ago when the first edition of this book appeared, e-commerce was just as impractical as it would have been in Hubbard's day. Today, however, it's a reality which has revolutionized Roycroft collecting.

Many of the prices noted in this edition are drawn from arts and crafts business web sites this writer visits periodically. However, the purely-Roycroft and non-commercial "The Webpage of The Roycrofters" (www.roycrofter.com) which greets visitors with a daily definition from The Roycroft Dictionary and provides a wealth of information and enjoyment for collectors and non-collectors alike, deserves a permanent bookmark and frequent visits. Over the years, it has alerted visitors to possible counterfeits, listed significant collections for sale and, via its bulletin board, delivered answers to a wide range of historical and collector questions.

Among important arts and crafts auction sites often including numerous Roycroft pieces are David Rago Auctions (www.ragoarts.com) and Treadway Gallery (www.treadwaygallery.com). Both post auction schedules and results and are linked with Amazon (www.amazon.live bid.com) enabling virtual bidders to participate in the literal auctions. Both sites also offer printed catalogs and other good information. eBay (www.ebay.com) is searchable by "Roycroft" and often lists at least 100 current items. Whether or not one chooses to bid, it is an excellent source of photo references. Among other photo and price sources are Craftsman Auctions (www.craftsman-auctions.com), Gallery 532 Tribeca (www.gallery532.com) and Jeffreys Royal Oak (www.jeffreyclay.com). Roycroft books, catalogs and ephemera may be searched at Advanced Book Exchange (www.abebooks.com), bibliofind.com or alibris.com among others.

For those who, like this writer, collect Roycroft items in order to connect with the history of the man and his institution, "dollars" can't describe their worth. A bookend, however attractive, is just a bookend until it is a piece of history, which is why this book connects the Roycroft's fascinating past with the present values placed on its wares. But there's no doubt that whether one chooses to call them values or to call them prices, the dollars being paid or asked for Roycroft objects have soared—but the ability to to locate, buy and sell electronically from a personal computer puts those prices in play, both literally and virtually, every day.

New to this edition, we have quoted current asking prices of Roycroft books on pages 26–28. Books in the "popular-priced" category which were bound in suede are delightful to own, but the more luxurious editions of the same title with hand-tooled leather bindings and hand-illumination and illustrations, will naturally bring much higher prices.

In Chapter 6—also new to this edition—we report prices, garnered online, for major categories of Roycroft collectibles discussed and pictured throughout the book. Some of the figures would have been unbelievable when the first edition of *Roycroft Collectibles* rolled off the press. Yet there are still bargains to be found so that even a collector on a budget may own a fascinating piece of history.

Introduction

Elbert Hubbard, "The Sage of East Aurora" and founder of America's Roycroft crafts complex, could trace his ancestry in this country to pioneer New Englanders who fought in the American Revolution. However, his interest in the past centered mostly on what early history could offer to his and future generations of Americans.

First a businessman with a flair for novel advertising schemes, he forsook the more conventional pursuits in 1893 to become a writer, philosopher, and active promoter of arts and crafts in America. Hubbard, more than anyone in his time, was responsible for the emergence of the widespread new interest in reading and the arts and crafts movement in America from 1895 to 1915 when he met his untimely death in the sinking of the S.S. *Lusitania*.

This was a period that left a legacy of imported interest in the crafts concepts of England's William Morris in everything from books to furniture making, to the emergence of Hubbard's own Roycrofters semicommune of artists and artisans in East Aurora, New York. Their output of finely printed and bound books, art, handmade copper, brass, silver, leather, and terra-cotta wares, plus Morris-like furniture, was, in retrospect, nothing short of phenomenal for a group that never numbered more than 500 persons.

Their works are treasured collectors' items which portray one of America's significant eras. But over and above the importance of these collectibles stands the importance of Hubbard himself, not only as a recognized leader in the arts and crafts movement in America but also as a sage and molder of public opinion here at the turn of the century. The result of this combination is that the collecting of Hubbard memorabilia of all sorts—almost anything directly or remotely related to the man—rivals the collecting of the output of his talented workers known as the Roycrofters.

Born in Bloomington, Illinois on June 15, 1856, son of country doctor Silas Hubbard and Juliana (Read) Hubbard, Elbert Green Hubbard grew up in what was then mostly prairie lands and never finished high school. By the time he was fifteen he had forsaken formal education and was in business for himself, peddling soap from a farm wagon, door-to-door, in Bloomington, Hudson, and neighboring Illinois villages. His source of supply was a cousin, Justis Weller of Chicago, who was in the soap manufacturing business with a former (and later to be again) Buffalo, New York soap tycoon, John D. Larkin.

In 1874, Larkin married Hubbard's older sister, Frances, and the way was paved for the ultimate partnership of young Hubbard with his brother-in-law in the formation of the John D. Larkin Co. at Buffalo in 1875. Hubbard was the junior partner, and his advertising and promotion programs had much to do with the early success of the Larkin enterprise in Buffalo and nationwide. There emerged from this alliance a burgeoning mail-order soap business that relied heavily on the incentives of Hubbard-devised club plan buying, premiums, and creative mailing pieces from the fertile mind and busy pen of Elbert Hubbard.

Later, after Hubbard had left the firm to start a new career, the Larkin organization, which had become almost as deeply involved in premiums as in soap, formed the spin-off Buffalo Pottery Company. That firm's dishes and ceramic wares have, themselves, become extremely valuable collectors' items. They are unrelated to the collecting of Roycroft items except for the distinctive china service they subsequently produced for the Roycroft Inn in the early 1900s.

It was in late 1893 that Elbert Green Hubbard dropped his middle name and sold back to Larkin his interest in what was by then known as the Larkin Soap Manufacturing Co. He had been bitten by the literary bug, having written and sold a novel, *The Man,* under the pseudonym of "Aspasia Hobbs." It had been bought and published by J.S. Ogilvie Co. of New York in 1891.

Hubbard had moved from Buffalo to East Aurora in 1884, had formed a chapter there of the Chautauqua Literary & Scientific Circle, and had secretly written his first novel while riding the daily commuter train between the suburban village and his business office in Buffalo. And, though he wasn't fully aware of it at the time, family man Elbert Hubbard had been bitten by yet another bug—the love bug.

Comely school teacher, high school preceptress, and temporary boarder in the Hubbard home, Alice Moore, had been his platonic but secret collaborator in the writing of *The Man.* She would ultimately become the second Mrs. Hubbard and be his strong right arm in his emerging role as "pastor of the flock" of Roycroft artisans, and his and their followers, known as the Roycrofters-at-Large.

The story of Hubbard's romance with Alice is a story in itself,* but she had much to do with the rise of Hubbard and the rise of the Roycrofters to national, and even international, prominence. And she made her own contributions to today's vast body of Hubbard/Roycroft collectibles.

Today's Hubbard/Roycroft collectors are almost as widespread and numerous as were the devoted Roycrofters-at-Large who looked to the Roycroft Campus as mecca and Elbert and Alice as their adored leaders. And, while the greater interest is in the nostalgia and in the beauty of the handsome books and carefully fashioned wares, plus the value of these and other Roycroft memorabilia, there is also a growing new interest in the philosophy expressed by Elbert Hubbard.

For the Roycroft/Hubbard collector, the period 1895 to 1915 seems to hold the greatest appeal. This period, covering the time span that embraced the formation of the Roycroft Shop in 1895 to the tragic deaths of Elbert and Alice in the *Lusitania* sinking by a German U-boat on May 7, 1915, was the most productive and most influential in terms of the Hubbard/Roycroft impact on the American scene. However, the Roycroft survived the loss of its inimitable leader, "Fra Elbertus," and lived on under the able guidance of his son, Elbert Hubbard II, until, in 1938, it became a belated victim of the Great Depression that followed the stock market crash of 1929.

There is considerable collector interest today in the 1915–1938 period and 1891–1895 pre-Roycroft period as well as in the major period during which Elbert Hubbard built and personally guided the destinies of the unique Roycroft organization. All are carefully covered for the collector in this work.

*Charles F. Hamilton, *As Bees in Honey Drown* (South Brunswick and New York: A. S. Barnes and Company, 1973).

1
The Hubbard Pre-Roycroft Period
1891–1895

The man who was to shortly establish a crafts complex in East Aurora, New York that was similar to the one of William Morris' at Hammersmith, England was, in 1891, not aware of where his great interest in art and literature would eventually lead him. At the age of thirty-five Elbert was busy finding himself . . . just as Morris had been at that age in another part of the world. But the paths of these men would soon cross and, while only in a brief and casual way, that meeting would completely change the course of Hubbard's life. It would also change the lives of many persons who knew or would come to know Elbert Hubbard.

Morris crowned his long series of successes in arts and crafts undertakings with the founding of his Kelmscott Press in 1890. In 1891, Hubbard had his first novel, *The Man*, published by J.S. Ogilvie Co. of New York, but it wouldn't be long before he'd follow Morris' example and establish his own press. Hubbard's several books, published by others prior to his setting up his own print shop, are the real, rare, and valuable collectors' items of the Pre-Roycroft period.

There is no known record as to how many copies Ogilvie printed and sold. It is known that, some years later, Hubbard burned a large quantity in his possession because he came to regard *The Man*

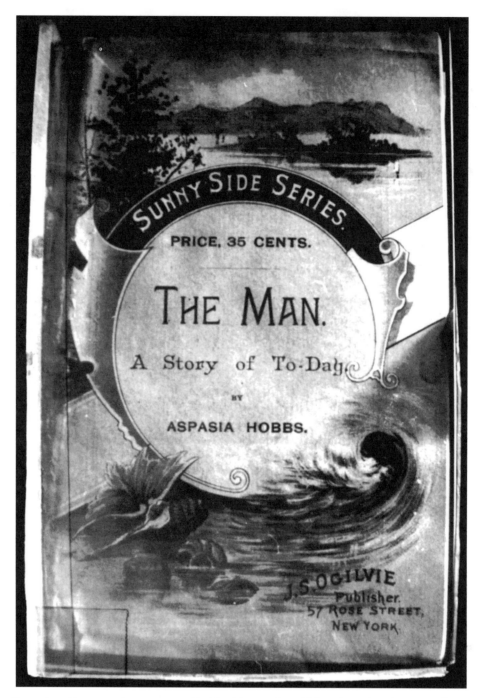

Exceptionally rare. The Man, *Hubbard's first novel and his only one under a pseudonym (Aspasia Hobbs). A paperback, it was published in 1891 by J. S. Ogilvie, New York.*

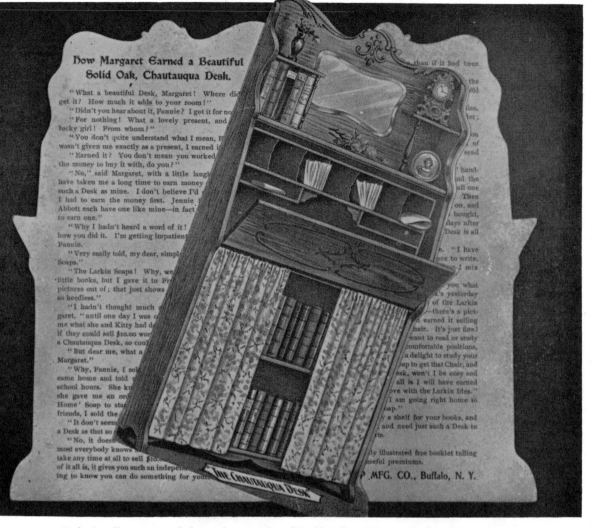

Today's collectors search for early examples of Hubbard's writing and advertising expertise. One such is this Larkin Soap Co. premium offer of a Chautauqua desk. A full-color, die-cut cardboard replica of the desk, it opened out to reveal a chatty Hubbard pitch for Larkin Soap.

as not a good example of his true writing ability. Nevertheless, it is his only literary effort written under a pseudonym and the only one written and published prior to his leaving the Larkin Co. to attend Harvard. Hubbard-Roycroft collectors have actively sought and found copies of this paperback book during the past decade with the result that at least five are now known to be in collections.

There are also collectors of Hubbard's advertising pieces for the Larkin Company while he was connected with that firm. Though they are unsigned, they are full of his unmistakable literary style.

After severing ties with John Larkin, Hubbard enrolled as a special student at Harvard for a year. And, though he was bored with the academic life, he did find there the time, research facilities, and inspiration to pursue further writing.

In 1893, he turned out, under his own name, a short story titled, *One Day* and, in 1894, a novel, *Forbes of Harvard*. Both were published by Arena Publishing Co. of Boston, Massachusetts. A

Hubbard's first novel under his own name was *Forbes of Harvard*. Published in 1894 by Arena Publishing Co., Boston, Massachusetts. Orginally issued in paperback, some were later bound in hardback, with the original cover included, and sold by the Roycroft Print Shop in its early days. The complete Roycroft collector seeks both issues.

William Morris, from frontispiece of Hubbard's book on the founder of the Kelmscott Press.

second novel in 1894, *No Enemy (but himself)* was published by G.P. Putnam's Sons, New York. As in the case of *The Man,* there are no known statistics on the printing runs of these three subsequent books, but current searches are bringing a few copies to light. Again, five copies of each are known to be in collections today and they rival *The Man* in rarity and high value.

It was in the spring of 1894 that Elbert Hubbard, long an admirer of John Ruskin, decided to go to England with the hope of meeting another Ruskin enthusiast, William Morris. But it was more than the common interest in Ruskin that caused Hubbard to want to meet the sixty-year-old artist, poet, author, manufacturer, and publisher. Here was a kindred spirit, and Hubbard wanted to emulate him and do in the United States what Morris had done so successfully in England. He was particularly interested in Morris' Kelmscott Press which, in a matter of just a few years, was already becoming world famous for its output of superbly printed, il-lumined, and bound books.

The two did meet and chat at Hammersmith. For Elbert Hubbard the meeting was all too brief, but that meeting and Hubbard's wide-eyed tour of the whole complex where varied arts and crafts were being profitably pursued caused him to want to hurry home to set up the beginnings of a similar enterprise in East Aurora. The

Elbert Hubbard at age thirty-nine when he abandoned a successful career as a soap executive to emulate William Morris as a leader in the arts and crafts movement. There was a striking appearance to both men and a strong resemblance about the eyes, nose, and mouth.

birth of an enterprise in America that rose to be viewed as a near religion, with many loyal followers devoted to Hubbard and the work ethic, was at hand. The "Roycrofters" would become famous and carve a niche in history.

Today more and more researchers of the pre-Raphaelite movement and the history of arts and crafts in America from 1895 to 1915 find themselves linking the names of Morris and Hubbard as men having similar influence in their times and spheres of activity. Morris is still the better known, worldwide, but it is interesting to note that Hubbard's Roycroft version of the "Morris chair" did much to direct America's attention to Morris' name and versatility.

Today's more frequent connecting of the names and work of these two arts and crafts figures undoubtedly has much to do with the revived interest in Hubbard and the Roycrofters . . . and the sometimes astronomical price tags affixed to Hubbard/Roycroft collectibles.

Aside from the like enterprises they founded, there were many other Morris-Hubbard similarities of a more personal nature. Both were striking in appearance; both had above average physical strength and energy; both affected unusual dress; they had a common love of the out-of-doors.

Morris loved to view architecture and historic sites; so did Hubbard. Both were omniverous readers as boys and men and had the same favorites in Ruskin and Carlyle. Both attended staid old colleges and were bored by the formalities of higher education.

Hubbard and Morris both became intrigued with Socialism at a time when they were financially quite comfortable, and they both eventually lost their enthusiasm for it.

The first noted signs of the writing talent of both have been traced back to literary efforts they mailed to their sisters. Both encountered marital problems.

And finally, in a long list of similarities, the crafts complexes of Morris and Hubbard emerged in much the same way—many of the items produced stemmed from an in-house necessity and later developed into manufactured products for general sale.

2

The Roycroft under Elbert Hubbard 1895–1915

Early Books

Inspired by his visit with William Morris, Hubbard came back to the United States ready to duplicate the art and atmosphere of Morris' work colony at Hammersmith. He couldn't do it all at once and, since writing was his first love, he made printing his first of many Morris-like projects to follow.

He founded in 1895, the Roycroft Printing Shop at East Aurora, New York. The name, he said, meant Kings Craft, but it is known that he admired the work of Thomas and Samuel Roycroft, early English printers, and owned some fine books done by them. He, therefore, may well have received the name inspiration from them.

On the Morris-Hubbard dissimilarities side, it should be noted that Morris' Kelmscott Press was nearly his last undertaking whereas such a venture was the beginning point for Hubbard's crafts complex. In passing, other dissimilarities worth noting were that Morris came from a wealthy family whereas Hubbard did not; Morris had artistic talents beyond writing but not so with Hubbard; Morris' principal associates in his business were men of equal talent and were his peers in the operation, but Hubbard began as a virtual sole proprietor and the talented persons he attracted to or de-

Hubbard's original printshop was the small, church-like building at the left. Then came the three-story addition (center), followed by another church-like addition. Trellis at extreme right was a part of Hubbard's home. The home, revamped, and these buildings eventually became the Roycroft Inn when Hubbard built new print and craft facilities across the street on S. Grove Street, East Aurora, New York.

veloped within his organization remained employees, albeit employees of a very paternal or fraternal employer, depending upon the degree of their talent.

The first book from the Roycroft Printing Shop was hand-set and printed on a Washington handpress. Its title was *The Song of Songs: Which is Solomon's; Being a Reprint And a Study by Elbert Hubbard.* The book was quite Morris-like. Hubbard's advertising broadside (reproducing, for its cover, the book's title page) is a collectors' item in itself. It sets forth, in Hubbard's own words, what was to become the book format and advertising styles that would ever after be characteristic of the Roycroft Printing Shop. It reads:

> The Roycroft Printing Shop, at East Aurora, New York, announces for immediate delivery an exquisite edition of The *Song of Songs;* Which is Solomon's; being a Reprint of the Text together with a Study by Mr. Elbert Hubbard, wherein a most peculiar and pleasant effect is wrought by casting the Song into dramatic form. The Study is sincere, but not serious, and has been declared by several Learned Persons, to whom the proofsheets have been submitted, to be a work of Art. The Volume is

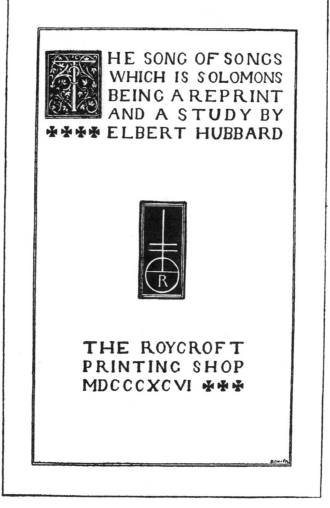

HE SONG OF SONGS
WHICH IS SOLOMONS
BEING A REPRINT
AND A STUDY BY
✦✦✦ ELBERT HUBBARD

THE ROYCROFT
PRINTING SHOP
MDCCCXCVI ✦✦✦

The cover of a promotional broadside for the first book of the Roycroft Print Shop's press was a reproduction of the book's title page. The broadside, like the book itself, is a valuable collector's item today.

thought to be a seemly and precious gift from any Wife to any Husband.

The book is printed by hand with rubrications and a specially designed title page after the manner of the Venetian, on Ruisdael handmade paper. The type was cast to the order of the Roycroft Shop, and is cut after one of the earliest Roman faces. Probably no more beautiful type for book printing was ever made, and, for reasons known to lovers of books, this publication will mark an era in the art of printing in America. This sheet shows the title page, size of leaf and quality of paper.

Only six hundred copies, bound in antique boards, have been made and are now offered for sale at two dollars each, net. In addition, there are twelve copies printed on Japan Vellum throughout, at five dollars each, but which are all sold. Every copy is numbered and signed by Mr. Hubbard. The types have been distributed and no further edition will be printed.

The book's colophon had a humorous touch, characteristic of Hubbard basic philosophy often expressed, "Get your happiness out of your work or you'll never know what happiness is!" It read:

AND HERE, THEN, IS FINISHED THIS NOBLE BOOK, BEING A STUDY BY ELBERT HUBBARD AND A REPRINT OF THE SONG OF SONGS: WHICH IS SOLOMON'S, TAKEN FROM THE HOLY BIBLE. PRINTED AFTER THE MANNER OF THE VENETIAN WITH NO POWER SAVE THAT OF HUMAN MUSCLE BY HARRY P. TABER, AT THE ROYCROFT PRINTING SHOP, THAT IS IN EAST AURORA, NEW YORK. BEGUN ON SEPTEMBER THE THIRD DAY, MDCCCXCV, AND FINISHED—THANK GOD!—ON JANUARY THE TWENTIETH DAY, MDCCCXCVI.

That colophon also set Hubbard's pattern for henceforth using that section of his books to give a pat on the back, now and then, to worthy printers, artists, and binders in his employ over the ensuing years.

The general style of this book demonstrated that Hubbard had well studied Morris' style. On November 11, 1895, two months after Hubbard had begun designing and setting up the first Roycroft book, Morris wrote an article to be read in America setting forth his aims in establishing the Kelmscott Press some five years previous. He said, in part:

I began printing books with the hope of producing some which would have a definite claim to beauty, while at the same time they should be easy to read and should not dazzle the eye, or trouble the intellect of the reader by eccentricity of form in the letters.

He went on to explain, that to accomplish these basic aims, he had to give chief attention to the form of type, the relative spacing of letters, words and lines, and the position of the printed matter on the page. He pointed out that, in his estimation, handmade paper should be used "both for the sake of durability and appearance." Morris further expressed a preference for Roman-style type developed by the great Venetian printers of the fifteenth century. What he wanted, he said, was "letter in pure form; severe, without needless excrescences; solid, without the thickening and thinning of the line," which, he felt, caused the more modern type then in use to be difficult to read. And finally, because he was a decorator by profession, he leaned toward suitable initial letter and margin decorations in his books.

Not being a decorator himself, and not having an artist-associate as talented as Morris' Edward Burne-Jones, Hubbard had assigned a difficult task to himself and his self-taught associates in trying to introduce a new "era in the art of printing in America;" the Morris-like era. But, in the *Song of Songs,* he did do just that and well enough to cause other American printers to follow suit and to have his pioneering efforts in this direction acknowledged, in due

Hand-illumining was a big selling feature of Roycroft books. Girls, trained initially by artist W. W. Denslow, were the principal illuminators. The "arty" and feminine touches to their workplace were much in evidence.

course, by the chroniclers of America's printing history.

The second book from the Roycroft Printing Shop also came forth in 1896. It was printed and bound in a style almost identical to the first. The size, 9½″ × 6¼″, was the same. Its title, also on a religious subject, was *The Journal of Koheleth* and was another Bible text reprint with a commentary by Elbert Hubbard. Seven hundred numbered and signed copies were printed and the type distributed.

The third book, issued in 1897, marked the first appearance of the shortened name of the enterprise. The Roycroft Printing Shop was now, simply, The Roycroft Shop. This book, still another in the religious vein, was *The Book of Job*. Smaller in size (approximately 8¼″ × 4¼″) and in the quantity printed (350 signed copies), its quality far exceeded that of the first two in every respect. It was beautifully hand-illumined in water colors and gold ink.

Today, these three specimens of early Roycroft are among the most difficult to find of all Roycroft books. It is not an impossible task but when they do show up in the hands of knowledgable bookmen, prices anywhere from $75 to $150 each are likely to be affixed. And the trend is ever upward because of the rapidly

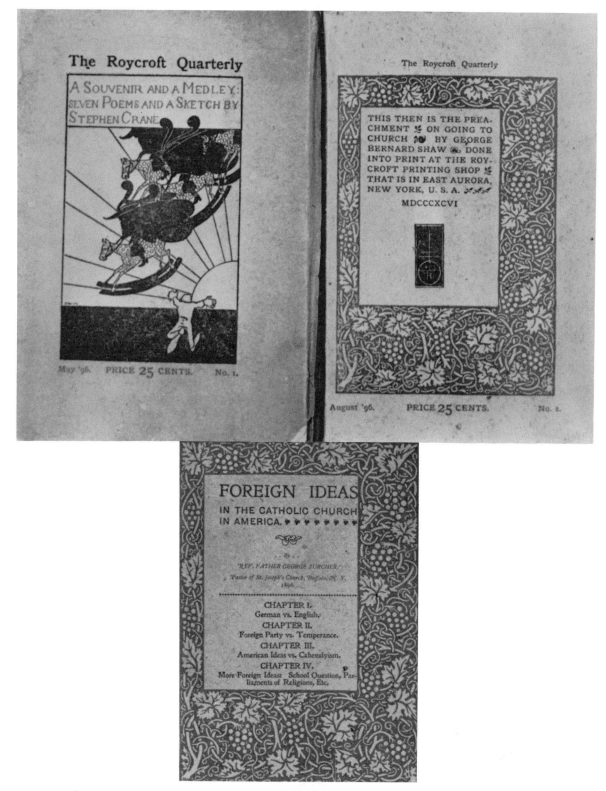

The three issues of Hubbard's only abortive magazine attempt, The Roycroft Quarterly. Issued in May, August and November of 1896 and then discontinued. The first two, devoted to works of Stephen Crane and George Bernard Shaw, respectively, are particularly prized today by Crane, Shaw and Roycroft collectors. May and August issues were 5" × 7½". November issue was 6½" × 9½" but the increased size didn't increase its reader popularity.

growing number of Hubbard/Roycroft collectors who grasp the significance of these pilot first editions which, incidentally, were priced a mere $2 to $5 at the time of their issue.

After these three early efforts, the output of the Roycroft Shop grew rapidly. And variant editions on special papers and/or in differing bindings came forth in such abundance for the next twenty years and beyond, that bibliophiles are still researching the total output. A typical example of the problems facing the researchers (which are, at the same time, the joys of the collectors) is the case of the Roycroft reprinting of George Bernard Shaw's essay, *On Going to Church,* in 1896. There are now known, through actual collection, at least six variant editions of that work, issued by the Roycroft Printing Shop. Comparison of the text in each indicates that all were printed from the initial typesetting and forty page layout format. The differences show up in the papers, bindings, title page styles and decorations, and the presence or absence of a colophon.

One of the six known extant editions is in paperback form and constitutes the only article in the August 1896 issue of the *Roycroft Quarterly.* The *Quarterly,* incidentally, was Hubbard's only magazine venture, among several, that proved to be an abortive effort. His later magazines (discussed elsewhere in this book) were huge and long-lasting successes.

The *Roycroft Quarterly* survived for just three quarters of 1896 but, partly because it was short-lived and therefore rare, and partly because two issues (May and August) were devoted to Stephen Crane and Shaw, respectively, individual copies command as much as $50 each today, with as much as $300 being asked now for a complete set of the three.

Although Hubbard wrote to Shaw, seeking permission to publish the essay in the United States and retained a postcard response granting such permission, the testy author-playwright later publicly claimed that Hubbard had altered the text here and there after agreeing to print it, "as is," as Shaw had requested. In his general ire and denunciation, Shaw further asserted that Hubbard was a poor imitator of William Morris. The feud, being a matter of record, has enhanced the collector value of the Roycroft edition of Shaw's essay.

As noted earlier, bibliophiles are still unraveling the facts and figures of Roycroft editions, including the printings of Hubbard's own writing and the works of other authors. Until their total and combined efforts are completed and published, the following limited bibliography for the 1896–1915 period will serve as a guide and starting point for Roycroft book collectors.

HE Master of the Roycroft Printing Shop desires to make the following announcements: ✤ ✤

✤ 1.—Beginning with the Book of Job, which is now on the press, all Roycroft books will be printed on "Whatman" hand-made paper.

✤ 2.—The minimum price of a Roycroft book will be Five Dollars, net.

✤ 3.—No Edition will be printed of more than three hundred copies.

✤ The Roycrofters employ no agents, neither do they sell through stores or dealers. All volumes are sent direct and on approval. Probably not more than four or five books a year will be turned out by the Shop, and to simplify delivery it is requested that book-lovers will allow their names to be recorded and volumes sent as issued. The following form of order is suggested:

"You may record my name for one each of your books to be sent on approval, express prepaid, as issued."

THE ROYCROFT PRINTING SHOP,
EAST AURORA, N. Y.

A·CATALOG OF ROYCROFT BOOKS AND THINGS YEAR ∴ TEN FROM·THE·FOUNDING·OF THE·ROYCROFTSHOP EAST·AURORA·N·Y

HE ROYCROFT PRINTING SHOP ANNOUNCE AS READY FOR IMMEDIATE DELIVERY

ON GOING TO CHURCH
By GEORGE BERNARD SHAW, author "Quintessence of Ibsenism," "Arms and the Man," etc., etc. (Authorized Edition.) This book is done throughout in the best Roycroft style: Romanesque type, Kelmscott initials, Dickinson's Dekel-edge paper, wide margins ✤ Price, stoutly bound in antique boards, One Dollar.

Twenty-five numbered copies on Tokio Vellum; special hand decorations on various pages done in water colors by Bertha C. Hubbard; bound in genuine vellum from skins prepared especially for us; price, Five Dollars, but are now all sold.

—THE—
ROYCROFT PRINTING SHOP,
EAST AURORA, N. Y.

✤

Price, per volume, $5.00. *The twenty-six copies specially illuminated by Bertha C. Hubbard, price $10.00 each, are all sold.*

THE SONNETS OF SHAKES-PEARE: On "Roycroft" paper. The initials and ornaments made especially for this book—hand illumined throughout. The price:

980 copies, bound plainly in boards, $ 5.00

Twelve copies on Classic Vellum, in
  full Levant—hand tooled, no two alike,
  each, All Sold   100.00

So far as we know this is the only book ever printed in America on genuine Vellum—the material being prepared for us by the man who supplied William Morris all the Vellum that was used by the Kelmscott Press. This edition was prepared with great care and is probably the nearest approach to a perfect book yet produced by the Roycrofters.

F THE five books issued by THE ROYCROFT the one that gives its makers most satisfaction is the *Ruskin-Turner*. The volume has been pronounced by a ✤ prominent member of the Grolier Club "the most artistic piece of bookmaking ever produced in America." The illuminations are all hand work, being done after the manner of the finest Sixteenth Century Missals. Printed in Romanesque type; nineteen ornamental initials, part of which are the Kelmscott, designed by William Morris, the others being our own designs. The Roycrofters are very glad to send their books "on approval."

"Kingly in its severe and simple elegance—it appeals to me as a genuine work of art. Your price for such a book I regard as merely nominal." So writes a member of the Caxton Club.

Through annual book catalogs, flyers and ads in Hubbard's magazines, he constantly promoted Roycroft books to his thousands upon thousands of fans. All these advertising pieces are collected today, principally as a means to identiy variant editions of Roycroft books, their quantities and special distinctions.

Roycroft Book Titles
(1896 – 1915)

Prices reported here are gathered from online sites of antiquarian booksellers and individual collectors, live auctions and Internet auctions as a matter of information, and not as an assessment of value. In addition to the condition of the book, consideration of variant–edition bindings, paper and illumination, limitation numbers, autographs and inscriptions, and provenance substantially affect asking or selling prices of the same title.

Dates and prices listed are for the first year of publication. Subsequent editions of some titles were produced in later years, both prior to and after 1915. The Printing Shop also produced various compilations and re–editions of *Little Journeys* throughout the period, as well as booklets, vanity and contract titles

Ali Baba of East Aurora, Hubbard, 1899, $125–225
American Bible, An, Hubbard, A., 1911, $12–100
Ancient Mariner, The, Coleridge, 1899, $40–215
Art and Life, 1896, Lee, $180–750
As It Seems to Me, Hubbard, 1898 —
As You Like It, Shakespeare, 1903, $45–250
Aucassin and Nicolette, Lang, 1899, $20–300
Ballad of Reading Gaol, The, Wilde, 1905, $35
Battle of Waterloo, The, Hugo, 1907, $36–750
Ballads of A Bookworm, Browne, 1899, $75–575
Book of Business, Hubbard, 1913, $23
Book of Songs, The, Heine, 1903, $19–175
Book of Job, Hubbard, 1897 —
Broncho Book, The, Crawford, 1908, $44
Chicago Tongue, Hubbard, 1900 — S45
Christmas Carol, A., Dickens, 1902, $50–85
Christmas Eve, Browning, 1899, $40
City of Tagaste, The, Hubbard, 1900, $120–275
Compensation, Emerson, 1904, $30–110
Complete Writings of Elbert Hubbard, 1908–15, $2950–5500
Confessions of an Opium Eater, DeQuincy, 1898 —
Consecrated Lives, Hubbard, 1904, $19–75
Contemplations, Hubbard, 1902, $35–1500
Crimes Against Criminals, Ingersoll, 1906, $120
Deserted Village, The, Goldsmith, 1898, $150
Dipsy Chanty, The, Kipling, 1898, $1000
Doctors, The, Hubbard, 1909, $51–70
Dog of Flanders, A, Ouida, 1906, $65
Dream of John Ball, A, Morris, 1898, $50–66

Dreams, Schreiner, 1901, $75–175

Essay on Friendship, The, Emerson, 1899 —

Essay on Nature, The, Emerson, 1905, $45–225

Essay on Self Reliance, The, Emerson, 1905, $40–100

Essays of Elia, Lamb, 1899, $70–250

Feather Duster, The, Reedy, 1912 —

Flush of June, Jordan, 1898 —

Four Gospels, The, Ricker, 1911 —

Friendship, Thoreau, 1903, $50–125

Friendship, Love and Marriage, Thoreau, 1910, $36–60

Garnett and The Brindled Cow, Hubbard, A., 1913, $100–200

Glynne's Wife, Young, 1896 —

Gray's Elegy, Gray, 1903, $50–71

Hamlet, Shakespeare, 1902, $40–100

Hand and Brain, Morris, Shaw, etc., 1898 —

Health and Wealth, Hubbard, 1908, $16–300

Holly Tree, The, Dickens, 1903, $65

Hollyhocks and Goldenglow, Hubbard, 1912, $75

House of Life, The, Rosetti, 1899, $195

In Memoriam, Tennyson, 1898, $125

In Memoriam, Roycroft Staff, 1915, $15–40

In the Track of the Bookworm, Browne, 1897, $35–$175

Intellectual Life, The, Hamerton, 1899, $275–350

Journal of Koheleth, Hubbard, 1896, $300–400

Justinian and Theodora, Hubbard, A. & E., 1906, $32–150

King Lear, Shakespeare, 1904, $54–275

King of the Golden River, Ruskin, 1900, $40–75

Last Ride, The, Browning, 1900, $375

Law of Love, The, Reedy, 1905, $30–65

Legacy, The, (2 volumes) Hubbard, 1896, $105–125

Liberators, The, Hubbard, 1915, $90

Life Lessons, Hubbard, A., 1909, $50–125

Lodging For the Night, A, Stevenson, 1902, $35–85

Love Ballads, unsigned poems, 1897 —

Love Letters of a Musician, Reed, 1898 —

Love, Life and Work, Hubbard, 1906, $65

Man of Sorrows, The, Hubbard, 1904, $20–450

Manhattan/Henry Hudson, Hubbard, Clark, 1910, $45

Maud, Tennyson, 1900, $35–95

Message to Garcia, A, Hubbard, 1899, (paper cover) $10–50

Message to Garcia, A, Hubbard, 1899, (suede cover) $185–450

Message to Garcia & 13 Other Things, A, Hubbard, 1901 $19–350

Mintage, The, Hubbard, 1910, $16–95

Myth in Marriage, The, Hubbard, A., 1912, $100–115

Old John Burroughs, Hubbard, 1901, $10–90

On Going to Church, Shaw, 1896, $50–225

On the Heights, Foote, 1897, $175–200
One Thousand and One Epigrams, 1911 —
Persian Pearl, Darrow, 1899, $900–2000
Pig Pen Pete, Hubbard, 1914, $27–46
Poems, Poe, 1901, $28–75
Respectability, Hubbard, 1905, $35–330
Rip Van Winkle, Irving, 1905, $117–250
Roycroft Dictionary, 1914, $30–46
Rubayiat of Omar Khayyam, Fitzgerald, 1898, $75
Ruskin-Turner, Hubbard, 1896, $80–458
Self Reliance, Emerson, 1902, $22–50
Sermons from a Philistine Pulpit, McIntosh, 1898, $100–200
Sesame and Lilies, Ruskin, 1897, $611
Song of Myself, Whitman, 1904, $71
Song of Songs, Hubbard, 1896, $360–575
Sonnets from the Portuguese, Browning, 1898 —
Sonnets of Shakespeare, Shakespeare, 1899, $375
Story of a Passion, The, Bacheller, 1901, $35–750
Story of Saville, The, Young, 1897 —
Time and Chance, (two volumes) Hubbard, 1899, $75
To Lovers and Others, Morse, 1914 —
Twentieth Century Musings, Burbridge, 1913 —
Upland Pastures, Knapp, 1897, $80
Virginibus Puerisque, Stevenson, 1903, $30–160
Walt Whitman, Hubbard, Stevenson, 1900, $40–95
White Hyacinths, Hubbard, 1907, $20–450
Will O' The Mill, Stevenson, 1901, $20–900
William Morris Book, Hubbard, 1907, $35–850
Woman's Work, Hubbard, A., 1908, $50–85

Note: Since the earlier editions of this book, we were among collectors able to assist Paul McKenna in viewing and documenting early Roycroft books and publications. His book, *A History and Bibliography of the Roycroft Printing Shop* lists known press runs. Variant editions, although unlisted, are still found. One likely explanation is that the print shop promoted custom binding and rebinding.

Another work of importance is David B. Ogle's forthcoming *On a High Shelf*, which documents numerous variant editions of Roycroft books and provides information on the materials, artists and craftsmen employed by the Roycrofters.

A MESSAGE ✖ ✖ ✖ ✖ ✖ TO GARCIA

IN all this Cuban business there is one man stands out on the horizon of my memory like Mars at perihelion.

When war broke out between Spain & the United States, it was very necessary to communicate quickly with the leader of the Insurgents. Garcia was somewhere in the mountain fastnesses of Cuba—no one knew where. No mail nor telegraph message could reach him. The President must secure his co-operation, and quickly.

What to do!

Some one said to the President, "There's a fellow by the name of Rowan will find Garcia for you, if anybody can."

Rowan was sent for and given a letter

This early 1899 edition of Hubbard's famous essay, A Message To Garcia, features W. W. Denslow's art and purports to be signed by the author. However, the signature on this copy is not Hubbard's. It was signed by a member of his staff with his authorization, a not infrequent practice at the Roycroft but not one that significantly affects collector value.

W. W. Denslow's sea horse version of the Roycroft trademark was employed as a watermark in the early imports of handmade paper from England and Italy.

Each of these books has a significance of its own and as a link in a total collection, but some have special aspects which make them more valuable as collectors' items. Certainly among those in this "special" category would be *Song of Songs, Journal of Koheleth, On Going to Church, Book of Job, The Dipsy Chanty,* the "homily" edition of *A Message to Garcia,* the manuscript edition of *A Message to Garcia & Thirteen Other Things, The Complete Writings of Elbert Hubbard,* and the complete bound set of the *Philistine Magazines.*

One thing is certain (based on a twenty-year study of the market for out-of-print Roycroft books) and that is *any* Roycroft-published book in good condition, and in the hands of knowledgeable dealers or collectors, can today command a price of no less than five dollars. Some, by virtue of their rarity, special history, special bindings, special illustrators (Denslow, Hunter, Barnes, etc.) can, and do bring prices of $75 to $150 and more. Bound sets of *The Philistine* magazine, depending upon the type of binding, can be worth as much as $350. The twenty volume *Complete Writings* which sold for $125 to $150 a few years ago is now occasionally seen offered at $400 to $600.

A word about Roycroft editions signed by Elbert Hubbard. All were manually signed but not all personally signed by Hubbard. Some were signed in his name, and in a style closely resembling his handwriting, by secretaries and officials authorized by Hubbard to do so in his absence. This happened only in the large-issue editions, for the most part, and/or in situations occasioned by Hubbard's prolonged absences from East Aurora on a lecture tour. This has not diminished collector interest in signed Roycroft editions. In fact, some collectors look for, and set aside in a special collection, the differing Elbert Hubbard signatures! Of course, the most prized signed editions are those with the authentic signature and, for the guidance of collectors we have reproduced in this book his actual signature from a copy of his passport application. Not to be overlooked, however, is the fact that any person's signature changes somewhat from writing to writing, from year to year, and depending upon conditions at the time of signing.

Finally, in this matter of collecting signed Roycroft editions, there is another interesting (and amusing) rarity to look for. In this author's personal collection of Roycroft books is a handsome, full-levant, modeled leather copy of Hubbard's *Hollyhocks and Goldenglow.* It is a 1912 first edition. On the flyleaf is printed this statement:

> The first thousand copies of *Hollyhocks and Goldenglow,* off the press, are numbered and autographed by the author, and this book is _____.

Inserted in the blank space, written in ink, is the figure 1162! Someplace out there in the collectors' world there must be 161 of

UNITED STATES OF AMERICA.

STATE OF *New York*)
COUNTY OF *Erie*) ss.:

I, *Elbert Hubbard*, a NATIVE AND LOYAL CITIZEN OF THE UNITED STATES, hereby apply to the Department of State, at Washington, for a passport for myself, accompanied by my wife, *Alice Hubbard*, and minor children, as follows: _____ born at _____ on the _____ day of _____, 1___, and _____, born at _____

I solemnly swear that I was born at *Bloomington*, in the State of *Ills* on or about the *17th* day of *June*, 18*56** that my (father) is a citizen of the United States, and I am domiciled in the United States, my permanent residence being at *East Aurora*, in the State of *N.Y.*, where I follow the occupation of *Publisher*; that I am about to go abroad temporarily; and I intend to return to the United States within *three* months ( ) with the purpose of residing and performing the duties of citizenship therein; and that I desire a passport for use in visiting the countries hereinafter named for the following purpose:

England
(Name of country.)   *Commercial Business*
(Object of visit.)

France
(Name of country.)   "

Holland
(Name of country.)   "

OATH OF ALLEGIANCE.

Further, I do solemnly swear that I will support and defend the Constitution of the United States against all enemies, foreign and domestic; that I will bear true faith and allegiance to the same; and that I take this obligation freely, without any mental reservation or purpose of evasion: So help me God.

Elbert Hubbard
(Signature of applicant.)

Sworn to before me this _____ day of _____, 19__

[Seal of Court.]

_____
Clerk of the _____ Court at _____

The authentic signature of Elbert Hubbard (reproduced here from his passport application in 1915) will guide collectors wanting to establish that their "signed" Roycroft editions were actually inscribed by Hubbard or by a staff proxy signer.

these over-numbered "signed" copies that were intended to stop at 1000!

All the more amazing and amusing to the collector is the fact that on the page opposing, is a photograph of Elbert Hubbard beneath which is a printed facsimile of his genuine signature. A quick glance from this facsimile to the ink inscribed signature on the opposite page quickly establishes that the latter is quite similar but not actually "autographed by the author!" Somehow, the amusing oddity seems to enhance its value as a collectors' item.

(Refer to chapter 3 of this book for a bibliography of books published by the Roycroft for the period 1916 through 1937.)

Early Magazines

The first magazine published by Elbert Hubbard was *The Philistine*. It was among the first, if not the first, pocket-size magazine of the many little "magazets" to spring up and become popular throughout the United States in the mid-1890s. Volume 1, Number 1 of the *Philistine* was published in June of 1895.

An overnight success, it continued in publication until Hubbard's death in 1915. The Roycrofters, recognizing that this particular

THE PHILISTINE

Vol. 1.   East Aurora, June 1895.   No. 1.

A Periodical of Protest.

———

Those Philistines who engender animosity, stir up trouble and then smile.   —JOHN CALVIN.

Copyright 1895.

PRINTED EVERY LITTLE WHILE FOR THE SOCIETY OF THE PHILISTINES AND PUBLISHED BY THEM MONTHLY.   SUBSCRIPTION, ONE DOLLAR YEARLY; SINGLE COPIES, TEN CENTS.

Vo. 1, No. 1 of Hubbard's popular Philistine *magazine. Its size was 4½" × 6"—a pocket size magazine. First appearing in June 1895, it was an immediate success.*

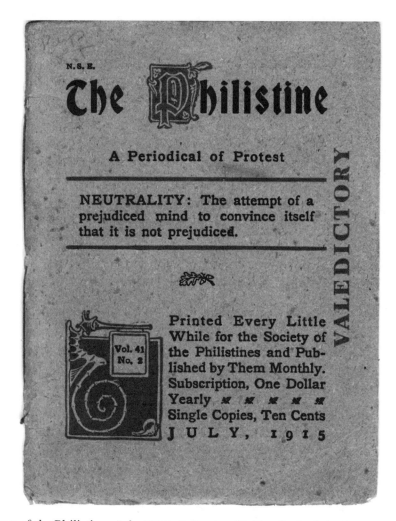

Last issue of the Philistine, *July 1915. Following Hubbard's death in the sinking of the S. S. Lusitania on May 7, 1915, the Roycrofters decided to discontinue it, knowing that no one could give it the personal Hubbard flavor that had made it so popular. "Phil" subscribers were switched over to* The Fra *magazine.*

publication's appeal stemmed largely from Hubbard's personal message in each monthly issue, discontinued its publication after issuing the June 1915 Anniversary Issue and the July 1915 Valedictory Issue.

Most notable of guest writers whose early efforts appeared in the *Philistine* was Stephen Crane, noted author of *Maggie, Girl of the Streets* and *The Red Badge of Courage.* But the greater portion of each issue was the literary outpouring of Hubbard, himself. It is perhaps the best continuing source of insight to the temperament and philosophy of Elbert Hubbard.

Hubbard fans had a habit of saving each and every monthly issue, and as a result it is still possible to find complete sets of the magazine covering the period of June 1895 through July 1915. Such loose-issue sets have sold recently for as much as $140.

Hubbard's classic essay, *A Message to Garcia,* first appeared in the March 1899 issue of the *Philistine.* That particular issue, alone or in

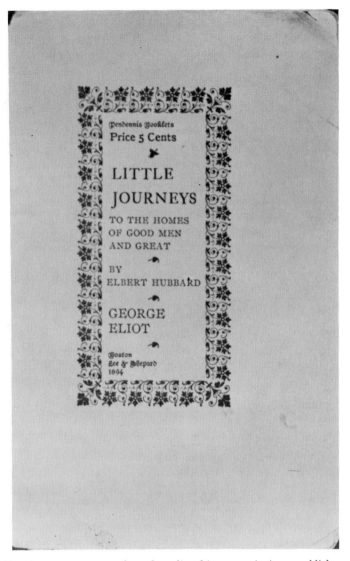

In 1894 Hubbard was a year away from founding his own printing establishment. He had a local job printer make up sample editions of his proposed Little Journeys *monthly magazine, printing different prospective publishers' names on the covers. Putnam's Sons bought the idea. Not so with Lee & Shepard of Boston . . . which makes this sample a unique collectors' item.*

the bound volume 8 of the *Philistine* is a much sought-after collector's item.

The second magazine to come from the Roycroft presses was the *Roycroft Quarterly* which has been discussed previously in this book in connection with the Roycroft publication of George Bernard Shaw's, *On Going to Church.* The three issues were May, August, and November, 1896.

The third magazine published by the Roycroft was the monthly *Little Journeys.* Each was devoted to a Hubbard-authored biographical sketch of a single famous person or couple in the arts, letters, or business. It got its start as a Roycroft publication in 1900 although from 1894 until 1900 the same magazine had been published (with

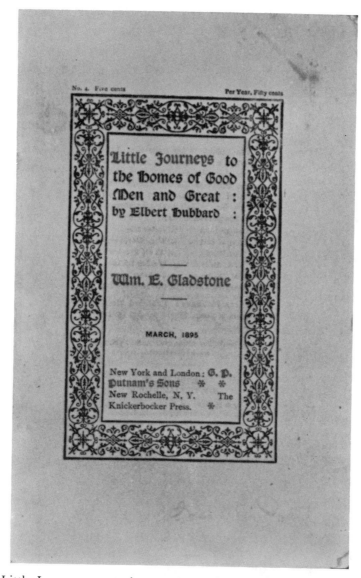

Hubbard's Little Journeys *magazine as originally published by Putnam's Sons. In this format it was 3¾" × 5¾". Hubbard took over publication of the magazine at the Roycroft in 1900, increasing the size to 7¾" × 5¾", and added frontispiece art by his staff artists (for the most part). While Putnam's Hubbard-written* Little Journeys *began in 1895, the original title and concept for the little biographical sketches dated back to an 1853 series issued by G. P. Putnam, predecessor to Putnam's Sons.*

Hubbard as the author) by G.P. Putnam Co. of New York. The *Little Journeys* continued as a monthly magazine from the Roycroft Print Shop until 1909.

These, too, were issued in bound volumes and the Miriam Edition of twenty-eight volumes is considered a collectors' item as are certain individual *Little Journeys* bound in limp leather or boards. In addition, collectors of Hubbard-related items seek both the individual Putnam issues and the five volume bound set of the Putnam series. Individual copies of these magazines of either period are bringing three dollars to five dollars each and the five volume set thirty-five dollars to forty-five dollars.

THE FRA

(NOT FOR MVMMIES)

A JOVRNAL OF AFFIRMATION

Vol. II.   JANUARY   No. 4

PVBLISHED·MONTHLY·BY·ELBERT·HVBBARD
EAST·AVRORA·ERIE·COVNTY·NEW·YORK
25·CENTS·A·COPY·2·DOLLARS·A·YEAR
THE·HVBBARD — ALBERTSON·DEBATE
■ "IS CHRISTIANITY DECLINING?" ■

23

Hubbard's FRA magazine, first issued in April 1908, was a prestiguous opinion magazine that was published monthly through September 1917. This January 1909 issue typifies the Dard Hunter style of cover design and the portrait sketching of Jules Gaspard. Both were full-time Roycrofters. Sketch was of Alfred Tennyson.

The fourth magazine to be published by the Roycroft was *The FRA*. Also a monthly, it first appeared in April 1908 and continued in publication for 113 issues through August 1917, two years after Hubbard's death.

The *FRA* was a large magazine (9″ × 14″) and the first issue carried the cover-page subtitle of *A Journal of Affirmation* whereas the little *Philistine* from the day of its issuance was called *A Periodical of Protest*. In some respects, however, the subtitles constituted a difference without a distinction because the editorial tone was strictly Hubbard. As a person he was known as "The Fra" long before his new magazine appeared with the same title. Thus, to some of his readers, the new magazine *was* the man, even more so than the *Philistine*.

Overall, though, the FRA was a much more sophisticated journal which opened its pages to more outside writers and subsequently began to carry a different subtitle, *Exponent of American Philosophy*. Between the covers of the *FRA* appeared articles on a wide range of public interest and concern, from alcoholism to womens' rights. It featured articles by and about captains of industry, educators, war, peace, prison reform—commentary on just about everything that was of then current interest. The famed criminal attorney, Clarence Darrow, was a contributor and subject, and a poet who was to become known and beloved as Carl Sandburg was an early contributor under the name of Charles Sandburg.

The biggest advantage the *FRA* had over the other Roycroft magazines was its page size which readily lent itself to the large-space needs of national advertisers. The *FRA* attracted the best: Gillette razors, Westclox, Kellogg's cornflakes, Wrigley's Gum, Studebaker, Steinway pianos, Chalmers, White trucks, Pebeco toothpaste, Armour meats, and a host of other manufacturers whose products were household words then and (some) now.

Significantly, too, the *FRA* became the instrument that launched Elbert Hubbard as a leading and unique advertising copywriter—a fact acknowledged by no less a personage than George Batten, a founder of the respected advertising firm of Batten, Barton, Durstine & Osborne. Hubbard originated the signed advertisement. He penned and sold to leading firms, such as those just mentioned, long, essay-type ads touting their products and signed each "An Advertisement by Elbert Hubbard." Indeed, they were the equivalent of signed testimonials by this man who had become internationally known largely as a result of his classic essay on initiative, *A Message to Garcia*. And, of course, each such signed advertisement for Elbert Hubbard who practiced well the initiative he well preached!

The *FRA* magazine is especially prized as a collectors' item for all of these reasons. They are a delight to old car buffs, to Hubbard buffs, history buffs, and to researchers digging into the early efforts of literary figures. In addition, persons interested in the history of advertising and the growth of the magazine industry in America find the *FRA* to be a significant link in their research chain.

Individual copies of the *FRA* sell today for as much as five dollars each. Like other Roycroft magazines, they can still be found and bound issues, though scarce and particularly prized, still occasionally show up at auctions.

(There were other magazines from the Roycroft Print Shop that were issued during the existence of the Roycrofters for twenty-three years after Elbert Hubbard's death. These, and their significance to collectors will be discussed in chapter 3 of this book.)

Crafts of the Roycroft

Printing and its allied crafts of book and magazine design, bookbinding, illustrating, etc. were, obviously, the initial and always important crafts in Hubbard's crafts complex at East Aurora. But, in much the same manner as occurred at William Morris' complex in England, other crafts entered the picture and grew in size, importance, and recognized excellence. As with Morris' enterprises, some grew out of internal needs and some out of the desire to widen the crafts horizon, not overlooking the widening of the commercial potential.

Those which emerged during the 1895–1915 period when Hubbard was alive and the driving and inspirational force of the Roycroft were the crafts that lived on (nurtured well after his death by his son, Elbert Hubbard II) until the venture folded in 1938, a belated victim of the Great Depression that had its roots in the stock market crash of 1929. Hubbard's early adoption of William Morris' philosophy of "Not how cheap, but how good!" also became the guiding force among the Roycroft craftsmen who took pride in their work and gave a truly special significance to the Roycroft trademark. Patterned after the mark first used by Cassiodorus in the Middle Ages, it was, to the extent possible, placed on every piece of work turned out by Hubbard's craftsmen who came to be familiarly known as The Roycrofters. The mark was the cross and circle which Hubbard divided into three parts signifying Faith, Hope, and Love. To it, he added the "R", to stand for Roycroft which their advertising blurbs stated was coined from roi craft, or Royal Craftsman, and interpreted further to be akin to Kings Craft. Perhaps Hubbard's admiration for the English printers Thomas and Samuel Roycroft and a study of the derivation of their family name resulted in the same conclusions for he certainly considered their work fit for a king. Whatever, it became a hallmark that stood for excellence in the eyes of those who acquired Roycroft items during the life of that crafts complex and means the same thing to today's collectors.

J. W. Mackail, in his 1899 biography of William Morris, reported, "The rooms in Red Lion Square were unfurnished; and from this trifling circumstance came the beginnings of Morris's work as a decorator and manufacturer . . . the arts of cabinet-making and upholstery had at this time reached the lowest point to which they have ever sunk . . . it was this state of things which drove Morris and Webb to take up the designing and making of objects of common use on their own account, and which led a few years later, to the formation of the firm of Morris & Company."*

Hubbard's plight was similar and even worse. He had no rooms whatsoever to accommodate the growing numbers of admirers traveling to East Aurora to meet and converse with him, a man grown nationally famous, almost overnight, as an essayist, philosopher, magazine editor, author, and book publisher. What he needed was an inn near his home and print shop and there wasn't one. He saw the need to build one . . . and did.

Hubbard's print shop was located a few hundred feet from his large Victorian home on the same side of the street. When he had the shop built in 1895 by local carpenters he asked for a churchlike frame structure, "like the little church at Grasmere" in England. By 1899, space needs had already dictated an addition at the rear which stood towerlike, almost overwhelming the original front portion.

He decided to erect several new buildings across the street; a "chapel" headquarters, a print shop, bindery, etc., all in a campus atmosphere. One by one they were completed within a couple of years from the commencement of work in 1899. Then with the transfer of printing equipment into the new buildings, he proceeded to build the Roycroft Inn, tieing in the old print shop with additions southward which eventually saw the engulfing of his old home. The Hubbards moved into a new home immediately south of the inn. The Roycroft Inn was open to guests by 1902. In general the inn resembled the architectural style of Frank Lloyd Wright, while the print and crafts complex across the street was studded with buildings that bore a marked resemblance to those at Kelmscott.

While a local carpenter-builder, James Cadzow, was officially referred to as the Inn's architect, just who really drew the plans for it and the much different buildings across the street still remains a mystery. Hubbard, unlike Morris, was neither gifted in design nor trained in architecture, but he knew what he wanted and was a good supervisor. Most likely, therefore, the buildings simply evolved with Hubbard telling local carpenters and stonemasons to "put this here and that there . . . and make it look like this."

The inn needed doors . . . big doors . . . and hinges for them. It

*J. W. Mackail, *Life of Wm. Morris* (London: Green & Co., 1899), p. 112.

Hubbard emulated William Morris even to the architectural style favored by Morris. Note the similarity in the Roycroft print shop and grounds to that in the accompanying old sketch of Kelmscott.

Soap executive Elbert G. Hubbard lived in this large East Aurora home, a portion of which was incorporated into the salon portion of the Roycroft Inn in 1900.

Early photo of The Roycroft Inn on S. Grove Street, East Aurora, New York. Little changed, it is still standing and operating as an inn.

needed lighting fixtures and leaded stained glass windows. It needed furniture and other ornamentations, including picture frames, art for the walls, and rugs for the floors. These needs were met in much the same way that Morris met them. He set his own people to work at making these things, hiring some new ones for their special talents, all mostly local talent. Similar needs for all of the buildings were met the same way.

By the time all of the in-house needs had been met, Hubbard had surrounded himself with talented, self-taught artisans for whose creative urgings he soon provided a ready and profitable outlet. And he urged them to continue to be creative in all of the arts and crafts they had learned, and even to try their hands at new ones.

Soon the Roycrofters became as well known for their furniture, wrought iron, copper, brass, leather, and other wares as they had been for their excellence in printing and bookbinding.

Furniture

The furniture was mission style and, of course, it was inevitable that the Roycrofters should introduce an American version of the

Furniture

OUR workers make the following pieces of hand-made furniture, in solid oak, antique finish. Medieval—modeled after the work done by men who made things just as good as they could.

FLAT TOP DESK, five feet long, thirty inches wide, six draws, $50.00

SOLID OAK CHAIR, very plain, not on swivel, to match desk, each, $20.00

TABLE, six feet long, three feet wide, mortised and pinned, $40.00

ALI BABA BENCH, bark side down, polished top, forty-two inches long, $10.00

MORRIS CHAIR, being a close replica of the original chair made by the hands of William Morris, cushioned complete, $50.00

BOOK CASE, five feet high, twenty-eight inches wide, bevel plate glass front, $35.00

ROYCROFT MAGAZINE PEDESTAL, hand carved, $20.00

SETTEE, high back, old fashioned, five feet long, held together with pin & slot, two draws under seat, $30.00

RAG RUG, hand-woven in three-yard lengths, $3.00

SERVING TABLE, 24 inches by 48 inches, $10.00

MUSIC RACK, $25.00

We further send the *Little Journeys* gratis, beginning with the current volume. Up to the present time twelve volumes of *The Philistine* have been issued, of which Volumes I, II, III, IV, V, VI, VII, VIII, IX and X have disappeared from Mortal View. We do not know where they can be procured. No number of *The Philistine* will be reprinted.

Sculpture

MADE from genuine East Aurora clay, as dug by Ali Baba from the bank by the dam-side, and modeled by St. Gerome in an Idle Hour:

Bust, in terra cotta, of William Morris,	$5.00
Bust of Fra Elbertus, three-fourths life size,	5.00
Bust, Study of " Ruth,"	3.50
Bas Relief of Franz Liszt, Panel Shape, 7x10,	3.00
Bas Relief of Walt Whitman, round, 9 inches,	3.00
Bas Relief of Fra Elbertus,	2.00
Bas Relief of Richard Wagner, Panel, 4x7,	1.00
Roycroft Paper Weight,	.50

Early price list of Roycroft sculpture. Note the reference to William Morris and the Morris Chair.

Morris chair. The finest oak and mahogany were used and the craftsmanship was superb. Small wonder that other hostelries around the nation sought Roycroft furniture and fixtures. One such was the beautiful Grove Park Inn at Asheville, North Carolina where sturdy Roycroft is still in use.

Roycroft furniture, bearing the distinctive trademark and/or the word, Roycroft, prominently carved in, is highly collectible today. Simple dining room chairs sell for from $100 to $200 each. Desk, tables, bookcases, depending upon size and condition, bring anywhere from $500 to $5000. Wood Roycroft picture frames, not all marked but unique in their mitering, and thus easily recognized by persons knowledgeable in Roycroft, are quickly snapped up at $50 to $150 depending on size and condition. They, too, were made of oak or mahogany.

There were also wastebaskets, bookends, clothes racks, carved motto signs, benches, footstools, china cupboards, buffets, etc., all made of wood. A simple taboret, for instance, recently sold for over $700! Individuals and museums are seeking all of them today and paying good prices for them—prices that would have not been dreamed possible by Hubbard and his craftsmen.

A Roycroft Interior

Sketch of "A Roycroft Interior" from a 1904 Roycroft Furniture Catalog shows such Roycroft wares as furniture, and irons, leather wastebasket, sculpture, copper trays and vases and hand-woven rugs.

Roycroft Furniture

IS not mission furniture. It's Roycroft and built roycroftie. Our styles are our own and our patterns are designed and developed right here.

We don't make a great quantity of furniture, but what we do make is made honestly by hand.

It will never wear out nor will you grow tired of it. The plain, simple, honest production never grows old and there is a satisfaction to be gotten from such things.

Perhaps if you intend purchasing a few pieces you better write us now, for if we happen to be out of what you want, it will take us four weeks to fill your order.

THE ROYCROFTERS
EAST AURORA, NEW YORK

Roycroft Furniture
For Christmas Presents

Furniture as a present is always acceptable

ROYCROFT FURNITURE intended for Christmas gifts should be ordered early as we carry no stock on hand.

Beautiful hand-made furniture (Roycroft) gives a joy to both the giver and receiver. Why not give a piece or two to those you want to make really happy? We have pieces for use in any part of the house. Our new Catalog shows some good things and if your wants are very special, let us know

Magazine Pedestal
18 in. sq.: 64 in. high
Price, $20.00

The Roycrofters Furniture Shop
In East Aurora, Erie County, New York

Roycroft Furniture

This Ladies Writing Desk speaks for itself. An ornament—convenient and useful—made in solid red oak—weathered finish. Price, Thirty Dollars. Our catalog will be sent on request.

The Roycrofters, East Aurora, N. Y.

Roycroft Rockers

¶When you invest in a Roycroft Rocker you assure yourself an Annual Dividend of Comfort for all the years to come. Roycroft Furniture lasts. ¶Round the Roycroft Inn many rockers just like this one have presented a sturdy and strong front to persistent usage for more than a dozen years. All sorts of Folks have helped us to polish these chairs, but the same workmen who made the first will make one for you, with the restfulness, rugged beauty and reliability unchanged.

No. 041. Rocking-Chair
21x19 1-2 in. Leather Seat, 38 in. high
Oak, $16.00   Mahogany, $20.00

THE ROYCROFTERS, East Aurora, N. Y.

Roycroft furniture was, and still is, classified as "mission" style of which Gustav Stickley of nearby Syracuse, New York was a leading designer and purveyor. Hubbard and Stickley were competitors and Hubbard chose to advertise the difference (which wasn't too perceptible).

Center Moriches, L. I., May 2, 1904

My Dear Roycrofters:

All of my furniture arrived in good time and in good condition—and it is quite impossible for me to write you how pleased we are. The stuff is certainly beautiful—every piece of it. There is not a single thing that I could suggest to improve it; it is far beyond our expectations, and I can assure you we fully appreciate all your kindness. Next season I will want the rest of the house furnished "Roycroft." I was foolish enough to have ordered a dining-room set before we saw yours, and while it is nice, at the same time, a comparison of the two different makes will be a great ad. for you. Enclosed find my check for $209, which, I believe, will settle our account in full, and I have never paid for anything more cheerfully. With all good wishes for you and yours from myself and wife, believe me to be

Most sincerely,

HARRY CLAY BLANEY

Typical testimonials from a 1904 Roycroft catalog.

Baltimore, May 26, 1904

The Roycrofters;

Gentlemen:—Enclosed please find my check for $201.25, payment in full of the bill for furniture shipped me by you. It gives me great pleasure to say that the furniture has surpassed my most sanguine expectations and I have taken delight in having my friends here examine the result of your handiwork. They are all lavish in their praise, and permit me to say further that I will be glad at any time to show the furniture to any one you may send to me. Some time in the near future I shall ask you to build me a hall piece; something on the order of a bench design, oval back and containing a mirror. When your art man has an odd moment, get him to sketch me a design.

Yours very truly,

WM. C. SMITH

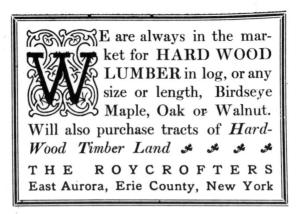

An ad in the Philistine *magazine every now and then kept the furniture shop well supplied with lumber and provided the chance for local and national mill operators and timberland owners to better their fortunes.*

Leather Goods

A spin-off from the hand-tooled leather bookbinding was a whole line of leather goods, all with the familiar Roycroft stamped in. There were bookends, wallets, boudoir slippers, manicure cases, stickpin and button cases, tie cases, cases for travelers' cups, pillows, photo cases and frames, desk sets, jewel boxes, card cases, watch fobs, womens' purses, table mats, room screens, collar cases, etc., etc., offered in the finest of leathers, expertly modeled in distinctive designs.

Since their uses were functional and therefore subjected to considerable wear, these more deterioration-prone wares are not as easily found today as the more durable Roycroft pieces. But they still show up now and then and have unusual value, particularly because of their scarcity.

Wrought Iron

Probably the least available and least marketable today as a collectors' item because they did not carry the Roycroft mark are the Roycroft wrought-iron products. They were among the earliest—and shortest-lived—Roycroft crafts products offered. Among them were andirons, fireplace hardware, ornamental light fixtures, flowerpot holders, etc. Recognizable as Roycroft today only if you happen to have an early *Philistine* magazine or Roycroft catalog by which a comparison of configurations, picture to piece, is possible, they are not otherwise significantly distinguishable from other manufactures of that day or later reproductions.

Copper, Brass, Silver

From the making of hand-fashioned door hinges and lighting fixtures and ornaments for the Roycroft Inn, to hardware for its

46

Close-up view of the reverse side of a Roycroft picture frame. The corners were lap-joined and not mitered as the scoring made them appear. (The white lines on the accompanying side view have been added to show the extent of lapping.) This construction is clue to Roycroft, with or without trademark.

furniture and trays and lamps to place upon tables and dressers, stemmed the manufacture of a wide and continuing line of copper wares for public sale.

A thick and crudely fashioned copper pin tray and a rather clumsy letter opener were the first items offered for sale at the Roycroft shops and in their 1906 furniture catalog. These very first issues from the Roycroft Copper Shop are extremely rare finds today and are highly prized collectors' items more because of their

Details of modeled leather designs in Roycroft pocketbooks. The trademark was generally stamped into the "ooze" leather lining of the purses, just under the clasp area.

Brass pencil holder and letter file from a desk set. Note the matching design lines. Circa 1913.

Unidentified artisans of the Roycroft blacksmith shop. Note the andirons and large chandelier in wrought iron. These were first made for the Roycroft buildings and later duplicated for general sale. The products were among the earliest in the crafts line offered by the Roycroft to the public.

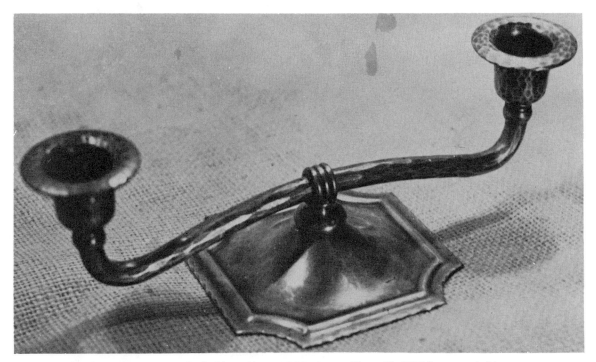

Hammered brass candle holder. Circa 1929. Base 4" × 4". Width across holder was 9½".

Copper tray. Note the Roycroft trademark in the center. Most pieces had the mark on the under side.

Roycroft dresser set; a hair receiver (right) and powder-puff box (left) in copper.

A Roycroft copper bud vase. It was 4½" tall. Base diameter was 2⅛".

Pocket matchbox holders at left serve as a size comparison for the miniature ash trays at right. They are made in copper and brass and came in hammered or etched finishes.

51

Roycroft copper and leather pieces from author's collection in display. Roycroft wares stand the test of time quite well.

Roycroft hat pin. Trademark was stamped on under side.

HAND-HAMMERED COPPER CANDLESTICKS—*For all Purposes!*

BOOK-ENDS IN VARIOUS DESIGNS
of Hand-Hammered Copper, done Roycroftie are just the proper thing for a Library or Reading Table!

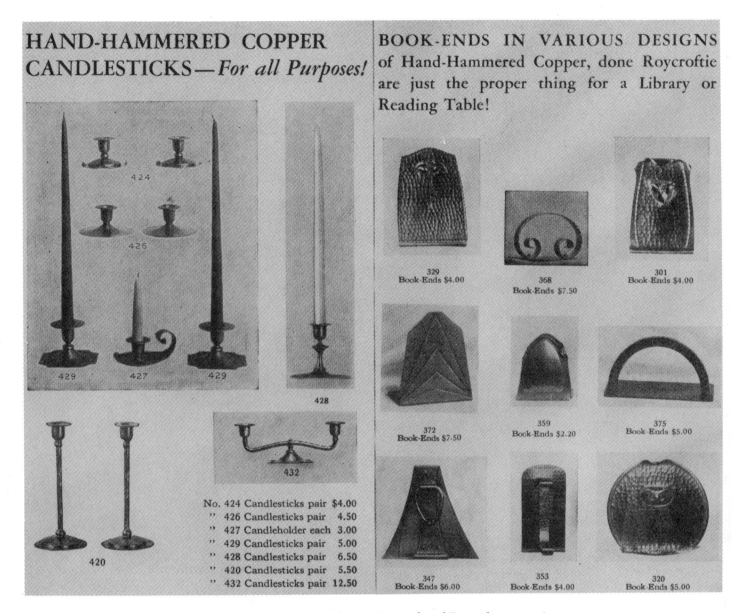

No. 424 Candlesticks pair $4.00
  ”   426 Candlesticks pair   4.50
  ”   427 Candleholder each   3.00
  ”   429 Candlesticks pair   5.00
  ”   428 Candlesticks pair   6.50
  ”   420 Candlesticks pair   5.50
  ”   432 Candlesticks pair 12.50

329
Book-Ends $4.00

368
Book-Ends $7.50

301
Book-Ends $4.00

372
Book-Ends $7.50

359
Book-Ends $2.20

375
Book-Ends $5.00

347
Book-Ends $6.00

353
Book-Ends $4.00

320
Book-Ends $5.00

Photo ads like these were always printed in the Fra, Roycroft *and* Roycrofters *magazines to tout the Roycroft wares. Today, next best to the complete Roycroft catalogs, they are the best identifying sources for collectors lucky enough to find them. These reproduced ad pages from some of those magazines give the collector a good idea as to the wide variety of wares and the resultant broad collecting potential.*

Baked
in English Ovens

Real English ovens were erected in Beech-Nut kitchens in which to bake these English Style Cream Crackers. And Beech-Nut cooks follow the very same recipe that made the original English cream crackers famous.

That's why Beech-Nut Cream Crackers are just as crisp and flaky as the imported variety. But there's this big difference—Beech-Nut Cream Crackers are *fresher* and *they cost less than half as much!*

Serve them with soups and salads. Order a package tomorrow.

Beech-Nut
Cream CRACKERS

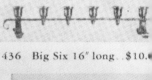

54

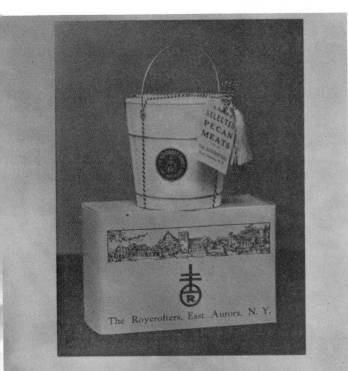

A ROYCROFT BUCKET
of selected PECAN MEATS

Made of Pine wood, this Bucket is unique and most attractive. It is 4¾ inches high and 4¾ inches in diameter at the top. It holds 7 ounces net weight and makes a delightful gift for anybody. The Pecan Meats in it are extra choice. Packed securely in an orange and black carton.

Price $1.35

THE ROYCROFTERS, EAST AURORA, N. Y.

Roycroft Handmade Copper

645—Handwrought Copper Ash Tray with two cigar rests and jade glass liner, 5½" in diameter
Price _____ $6.00

663—Three Bookish Copper Containers for cigarettes.
Price_____$10.00

372—Copper Bookends onlays on brass 5" high. Price $7.50
373—Copper Bookends onlays on nickel-silver, 5" high.
Price _____ $9.00

250—Copper Bowl 6" in diameter.
Price_____$4.00

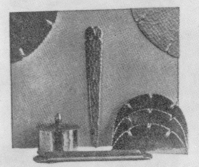

722—Desk Set of 5 pieces: Desk Pad, Stationery Holder, Ink Cup, Pen Tray, Paper Knife. Price _____$17.50

218—Copper Vase 5½" high.
Price ___ $5.00

THE ROYCROFTERS, EAST AURORA, N. Y.

1923

THE ROYCROFT SHOP IN EAST AURORA

A · CATALOG · OF BOOKS · & · THINGS HAND · MADE · AT THE ROYCROFT · SHOPS

VASE—C-201—$10.00
Height, 19 inches

C-903—$15.00
Roycroft Lamp of Hand-Wrought
Copper Equipped for Electricity
Height, 14 inches

ROYCROFT BOWL
C-208—Diameter, 10½ inches, $5.00
C-209—Diameter, 13½ inches, 9.00

VASE
C-108
$2.00
Height
8 inches

C-602
MATCH-HOLDER
WITH TRAY
$2.00
Height, 3½ inches

C-102
VASETTE
50 Cents
Height
4 inches

C-801—NUT-SET—COMPLETE, $10.00

C-701—DESK-SET—COMPLETE, $12.00

C-1103—CHAFING-DISH—$20.00
Tray, 14 inches in diameter—Height, over all, 8 inches

A Roycroft catalog. Sometimes wares and book offerings were combined in a single catalog. Generally they issued one for furniture, another for books, and still another for all other items. Mostly on an annual basis, they were sent free but in today's collector market sell for $25 to $45 each. Those with Dard Hunter cover designs command the higher prices. All with many photos, measurements, descriptions, and original prices, the catalogs are excellent guides for collectors.

scarcity than the quality of workmanship. It wasn't until about 1909 that a truly well organized and talented Copper Shop group began turning out the fine specimens of the craft. But from then on, until the Roycroft folded in 1938, their output was amazingly large for a handcrafted line. The variety of products grew and grew and the quality was superb. They worked in copper, brass, silver, silver plate, and etched silver and brass.

At times they combined metal with glass (Corning Stueben, no less!), the latter being utilized for lamp stems, shades, and for bud vases and candle holders. Naturally, today, these combination items bring the highest prices for they are two collectibles in one—Roycroft and the much-sought Stueben. The range is $250 to $800 currently depending upon the pieces.

A real gem to look for! Roycroft copper holder with vase in Stueben Bubbly glass from Corning Glass Co. (center of ad)

ROYCROFT LAMPS

902—Shade of Copper and Tortoise, 15 in. high $25.00
906—Desk Lamp, Copper Shade 13 in. high 12.50
919—Shade of Stueben Rosa Moss Agate Glass, 15¾ in. high 25.00

Charges   Prepaid

Some Roycroft lamps. There were many other styles. Note that shade for lamp at lower left was Stueben Moss Agate, making it particularly valuable today.

In the beginning, Roycroft copper, brass, silver (and leather and books) wares were sold only on the Roycroft campus and by mail through ads in Hubbard's various magazines and annual catalogs. And, though these methods continued during the life of the Roycroft enterprises, an added outlet was opened in November, 1915, following Elbert Hubbard's death in May of that year.

The Roycrofters put it this way in a letter to department and gift store managers in the United States:

The Roycrofters have decided to modify their Sales Policy. Heretofore we have sold Roycroft handmade Goods, Books, Leather, Copper, etc., to the extent approximating half a million dollars a year, *by Mail!*

Now we have decided to offer Roycroft Books, Leather and Copper in High Grade Stores. The Roycroft Products are unequaled, the finest of their kind made in America. They have won prizes in all the Art Centers: Paris, Antwerp, Berlin and London.

This Institution, founded by Elbert Hubbard, has been established twenty-one years. In every important city of the United States thousands of people have subscribed to our magazines, *The Philistine* and *THE FRA!* Tremendous prestige and goodwill is definitely established.

The Roycroft Copper Shop craftsmen assembled for this group photo in early 1900s. At extreme left is Karl Kipp, the master craftsman who became the first head of the shop.

The purpose of this letter is to ask you, would you be interested in ordering and suitably displaying Roycroft Goods? Would you be interested in organizing, perhaps a small Roycroft Department or "Corner" in your store?

The letter went on to explain that prices to the stores would be 33 percent off catalog retail prices, plus an additional 2% for cash in ten days; that they would not be placed on a consignment basis, and that the Roycrofters would sell to only one store in a city.

Almost overnight twelve major stores throughout the United States bought the idea, mostly in the Northeastern quarter of the country. Eventually they numbered several hundred. Among the early ones on the bandwagon were Lord & Taylor, New York; Marshall Field & Co., Chicago; Stix, Baer & Fuller Co., St. Louis; Joseph Horne & Co., Pittsburgh; Wm. Hengerer Co., Buffalo; and others of similar prestige.

The "carry homes" from visits to the Roycroft Campus and the mail order sales had well scattered the Roycroft wares to the remote hamlets all over the United States. But with the advent of the larger quantity sales through major stores in major cities an inadvertent later boon to Roycroft collectors was created. These stores had *bought* the wares. They weren't there on consignment, to be re-

Copper finishing section of the early Roycroft Copper Shop, or "department" as it was called internally. Women as well as men were employed here but the fashioning was done by males.

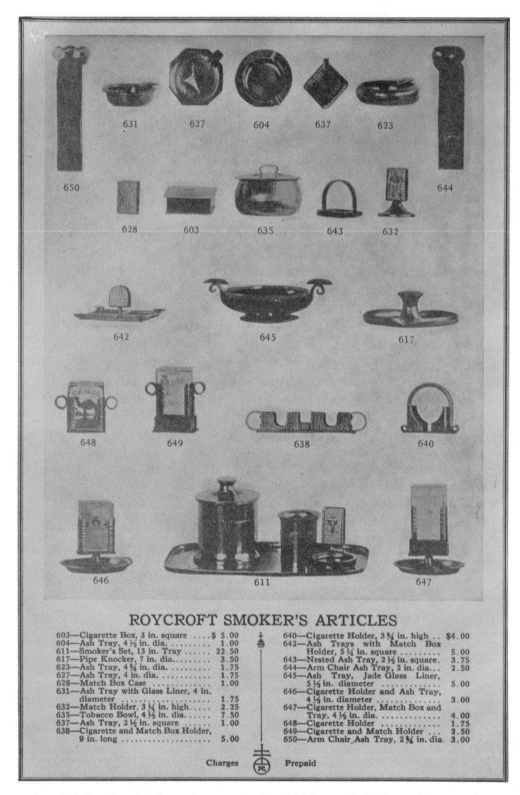

ROYCROFT SMOKER'S ARTICLES

603—Cigarette Box, 3 in. square ....$ 5.00
604—Ash Tray, 4 ½ in. dia. 1.00
611—Smoker's Set, 13 in. Tray 22.50
617—Pipe Knocker, 7 in. dia......... 3.50
623—Ash Tray, 4 ¾ in. dia. 1.75
627—Ash Tray, 4 in. dia. 1.75
628—Match Box Case 1.00
631—Ash Tray with Glass Liner, 4 in.
    diameter 1.75
632—Match Holder, 3 ¼ in. high..... 2.25
635—Tobacco Bowl, 4 ½ in. dia. 7.50
637—Ash Tray, 2 ½ in. square 1.00
638—Cigarette and Match Box Holder,
    9 in. long 5.00

640—Cigarette Holder, 3 ¾ in. high .. $4.00
642—Ash Trays with Match Box
    Holder, 5 ¼ in. square 5.00
643—Nested Ash Tray, 2 ½ in. square. 3.75
644—Arm Chair Ash Tray, 2 in. dia... 2.50
645—Ash Tray, Jade Glass Liner,
    5 ½ in. diameter 5.00
646—Cigarette Holder and Ash Tray,
    4 ½ in. diameter 3.00
647—Cigarette Holder, Match Box and
    Tray, 4 ½ in. dia. 4.00
648—Cigarette Holder 1.75
649—Cigarette and Match Holder ... 2.50
650—Arm Chair Ash Tray, 2 ¾ in. dia. 3.00

Charges   Prepaid

*An ad designed to delight smokers ran in the 1926 issues of the Roycrofter magazine.
Ironically, founder Elbert Hubbard lectured and pamphleteered on the evils of smoking!*

ROYCROFT HAND-MADE THINGS

Akron, Ohio	Foster Roberts Gift shop
Alameda, Calif.	Corvin Bros., 1358 Park Street
Allentown, Pa.	Summy & Werner, 924 Hamilton Street
Alton, Ill.	J. H. Booth, Jeweler
Altoona, Pa.	Wm. F. Gable & Co. Dept. Store
Ann Arbor, Mich.	Chas. W. Graham, Books & Stationery
Anaheim, Calif.	E. D. Abrams, Stationery
Appleton, Wis.	Ryan's Art Store, 584 Oneida Street
Ardmore, Okla.	Riegelman Jewelry Co.
Ardmore, Pa.	J. E. Barkman, Gift Shop
Asheville, N. C.	Grove Park Inn
Athens, Ohio	Logan's Book Store
Atlantic City, N. J.	Foster & Reynolds, Boardwalk
Atlantic City, N. J.	Foster & Reynolds Co., Haddon Hall
Auburn, N. Y.	Edgar S. & Frank A. Jennings, Art Store
Aurora, Ill.	Trask & Plain
Austin, Texas	University of Texas Co-operative Society
Baltimore, Md.	Hutzler Bros., Department Store
Batavia, N. Y.	MacGreevey-Sleght-De Graff Co.
Bath, N. Y.	Charles Kausch, Jeweler
Battle Creek, Mich.	Austin & Co., Glassware
Bellaire, Ohio	J. C. McKelvey, Jeweler
Berkeley, Calif.	Sather Gate Book Shop. Telegraph Avenue
Berkeley, Calif.	J. F. Hink & Son, Inc., Dry Goods
Berkeley, Calif.	Wurts Gift Shop, 2500 Bancroft Way
Binghamton, N. Y.	Fowler, Dick & Walter
Birmingham, Ala.	Reid Lawson Co., Jewelers, First National Bank Bldg.
Bisbee, Ariz.	L. R. Brehm Jewelry Co.
Bloomington, Ill.	W. B. Read Co., Books & Stationery
Boston, Mass.	M. T. Bird & Co., Stationers, 5-7 West Street
Boulder, Colo.	Co-operative Store, University of Colorado
Bradford, Pa.	B. G. Robertson, China
Bridgeport, Conn.	D. N. Read., Department Store
Brookings, S. D.	E. H. Beatty, Jeweler
Brooklyn, N. Y.	Anthony's Inc., 293 Livingston Street
Buffalo, N. Y.	The Wm. Hengerer Co., Department Store
Burlington, Vt.	Hobart J. Shanley
Butte, Mont.	Mrs. W. W. Talbot, Gift Shop
Cambridge, Ohio	Slingluff's Book & Gift Store
Casper, Wyoming	Casper Stationery Co.
Cedar Rapids, Iowa	A. C. Taylor & Son, Jewelers
Champaign, Ill.	University of Illinois Supply Store
Charleston, W. Va.	C. I. Coffey Book Store
Charlottesville, Va.	Anderson Bros.
Chattanooga, Tenn	T. H. Payne & Co., Booksellers
Chautauqua, N. Y.	Helen M. Bailey
Chester, Pa.	The Cross Co.
Chicago	Brentano's
Chicago	Quest Gift Shop, 7653 North Pauline Street
Chicago	The Holmes Co., Stationers, 17 N. State Street
Chicago	University of Chicago Book Store, Ellis Avenue
Chicago	The Stoner Co., 15 E. Washington
Chicago	The Tobey Furniture Co.
Cincinnati, Ohio	H. & S. Pogue Co., Department Store
Clarksburg, W. Va.	Struve & Giles Co.
Cleveland	Burrowes Bros. Co., Books
Cleveland	Kinney & Levan Co., China & Glassware
Cleveland	Korner & Wood Co., Art-Stationery-Books
Cleveland	Squier Work Shop, Euclid and 97th St.
Cleveland	University Book Store, 10514 Euclid Avenue

Beauty and utility wedded—that is what ROYCROFT Hand-made things in Leather and Copper are! If there is a Roycroft Shop in your town, visit it. You'll be delighted.

From 1915 (when the Roycrofters first began marketing their wares through retailers instead of via direct mail) to 1924, the list of stores selling Roycroft throughout the nation grew to over 320. Originally, there was to be only one authorized franchise in each major city but, as this published list indicates, the policy underwent change. Today the list provides as many clues as to cities where old Roycroft might be found as it did for locating them as new products.

Coldwater, Mich.	Sarah E. Fisher, Gift Shop, 63 Church Street
Columbus, Ohio	Pettibone McLean Co., Hartman Theatre Bldg.
Columbus, Ohio	College Book Store, 1836 N. High Street
Cooperstown, N. Y.	M. F. Augur
Corvallis, Ore.	O. A. C. Co-operative Association
Covina, Calif.	Covina Book & Art Store
Dallas, Tex.	J. D. Van Winkle, Books, 1711 Elm Street
Danville, Ky.	E. H. Kahn, Jewelry
Danville, Ill.	Straus & Louis Co., Department Store
Dayton, O.	Pettibone-McLean Co., Books, 23 W. 2nd Street
Daytona, Fla.	L. H. Rowe & Co., Jewelers
Decatur, Ill.	Haines & Essick, Books & Stationery
De Kalb, Ill.	Orno Shop, H. R. Sorensen
Denver, Colo.	W. H. Kistler Stationery Co.
Denver, Colo.	Daniels & Fisher Stores Co.
Des Moines, Iowa	Younker Bros., Department Store
Detroit	Bleazby Shop of Gifts, 31 East Adams Avenue
Douglass, Ariz.	W. H. Brannan, Jeweler
Dubuque, Ia.	Hopkins & Witty, Jewelers
Duluth, Minn.	Eva Hooker Drake's Shop
Dunkirk, N. Y.	Dunkirk China Shop, 341 Main Street
Elmira, N. Y.	MacGreevy-Sleght-DeGraff Co., Books & Stationery
El Paso, Tex.	Popular Dry Goods Co., Department Store
Ely, Nevada	W. H. Bishop, Jeweler
Enid, Okla.	McConkey Art & Gift Shop
Elyria, Ohio	Miss E. N. Johnston, Gift Shop, 230 2d Street
Erie, Pa.	Therese J. Ballard, 27 W. 7th St.
Estes Park, Colo.	The Gracraft Shop
Eugene, Ore.	W. A. Elkins, The Gift Shop
Evanston, Ill.	H. E. Chandler & Co., University Book Store
Fairmont, W. Va.	Holt Rowe Novelty Co.
Fayetteville, Ark.	Ozark Art & Gift Shop
Fitchburg, Mass.	Nichols & Frost, 341-357 Main
Flint, Mich.	C. M. Brownson, Art Goods, 625 S. Saginaw
Fort Wayne, Ind.	Robert Koerber, Jeweler, 816 Colhoun
Fostoria, O.	The Book Shop
Freeport, Ill.	Fargher's Book & Gift Shop
Fremont, Neb.	Hjalmar Anderson, Jeweler
Fresno, Calif.	Byfield's Shop of Gifts, Tulare Street
Galesburg, Ill.	Stromberg & Tenney, Books, Art Goods
Galveston, Texas	The Gift Shop, 2110 Avenue E
Geneva, N. Y.	L. H. Barth, Jewelry, Art Goods
Globe, Ariz.	The Mine Supply & Hardware Co.
Grand Haven, Mich.	Reichardt Book Store
Grand Island, Neb.	August Meyer & Son, Jewelers
Grand Junction, Colo.	Outing Shop
Grand Rapids, Mich.	Bluebird Gift Shop
Great Falls, Mont.	Strain Bros. Department Store
Greeley, Colo.	Geo. D. Horne, Book Store
Greenville, N. C.	W. L. Best, Jeweler
Greensboro, N. C.	Wills Book & Stationery Co.
Hamilton, O.	Spellman's
Harrisburg, Pa.	Art & Gift Shop, 105 Second Street
Hartford, Conn.	Mrs. Helen R. Marvin, Gift Shop, 55 Pratt Street
Helena, Mont.	A. P. Curtin
Herkimer, N. Y.	H. G. Munger & Co.
Hershey, Pa.	Hershey Dep't Store.
Houghton, Mich.	Matt Haug, Jeweler
Houston, Tex.	Cargill Co., Stationers, 409 Fannin Street
Huntington, W. Va.	C. M. Wallace & Son, Jewelers
Independence, Ore.	Craven & Walker
Indianapolis, Ind.	Beach's Bookstore, Spink Arms Hotel
Iowa City, Iowa	Mathieson & Shuck, Book & Crafts Shop

ROYCROFT Handmade things in Leather and Copper solve the gift problem.
The Roycroft Shop in your town is for your convenience. Use it.

Ithaca, N. Y.	Little Crafts Shop, 201 N. Aurora St., Louis D. Neill
Jackson, Mich.	The China Shop, 119 W. Main
Jamestown, N. Y.	Abrahamson-Bigelow Co., Department Store
Jerome, Ariz.	C. C. Robinson, Jeweler
Johnstown, Pa.	Rothsteins, Jewelers
Joliet, Ill.	Henley-Relyea Co , Books, 132 N. Ottawa
Kankakee, Ill.	The Alice Gift Shop
Kansas City, Mo.	Emery-Bird-Thayer Co.
Kingston, N. Y.	W. S. McDonough
La Fayette, Ind.	O. L. Foster Sup. Shop
Lake Placid, N. Y.	Lake Placid Club Stores
Lancaster, Pa.	Darmstaetter's Gift Shop, 59 N. Queen
Lansing, Mich.	Heath's Jewelry Store
Lebanon, Ore.	Sigurd Landstrom, Jeweler
Lexington, Ky.	Transylvania Printing Co.
Lima, Ohio.	C. E. Schell
Lincoln, Neb.	Rudge & Guenzel, Department Store
Lockport, N. Y.	Harry Hamil, Jeweler, 77 Main Street
Lodi, Calif.	F. S. Sigfried, Stationery
Long Beach, Calif.	Hewitt's Book Store
Los Angeles, Calif.	Broadway Department Store
Los Angeles, Calif.	Bullock's
Los Angeles, Calif.	Fowler Bros., Books, South Broadway
Los Angeles, Calif.	A. E. Little Co., Art Shop, 426 S. Broadway
Los Angeles, Calif.	Rogers Stationery & Art Store, Western Avenue
Los Angeles, Calif.	Westlake Art Shop, 694 So. Alvarado
Los Angeles, Calif.	White's Photo Art Shop, 5628 Pasadena Ave.
Lowell, Mass.	Bon Marché Co.
Lynchburg, Va.	J. P. Bell & Co.
Madison, Wis.	K-K Shop, 606 State Street, Gift Shop
Mansfield, Ohio	O. P. Crouse Co., Gift Shop
Marietta, Ohio	Charles Sugden Book Store
Marysville, Calif.	Leo J. Smith, Jeweler
Morristown, N. J.	Frank S. Burnett, Art Goods, 15 South Street
Marquette, Mich.	Schoch & Hallam, Jewelers, 214 S. Front Street
Marshfield, Ore.	Belding & Bushong, Jewelers, 220 Central Ave.
Medford, Ore.	Medford Book Store
Memphis, Tenn.	Memphis Photo Supply Co., 60 S. Main
Memphis, Tenn.	Louise Fleece Gift Shop
Meriden, Conn.	Gibson Art & Gift Shop, 59 W. Main Street
Miami, Florida	Foster & Reynolds Co.
Milwaukee, Wis.	H. W. Brown & Co., Gift Shop, 87 Wis. Street
Middletown, Ohio	The Book Shop, 116 E. Third Street
Minneapolis	Mrs. Emily Singer, Gift Shop
Minneapolis	Powers Merc. Co., Department Store
Modesto, Calif.	Lee Bros. Stationery
Monrovia, Calif.	Glenn L. Box
Montclair, N. J.	E. Madison Co., Art Goods, 427-429 Bloomfield Ave.
Montgomery, Ala.	C. L. Ruth & Son, Jewelers, 15 Dexter Avenue
Morristown, N. J.	Frank S. Burnett, 15 South Street
Mount Morris, N. Y.	A. H. Jenks & Son, Jewelers
Muncie, Ind.	C. A. Penzel
Muskegon, Mich.	The Daniels Co.
Nashville, Tenn.	R. M. Mills Book & Gift Shop, 623 Church Street
Newark, N. J.	Fred'k Keer's Sons, Art Store, 917 Broad
New Bedford, Mass.	H. S. Hutchinson, Books & Stationery, 222-226 Union St.
Newburgh, N. Y.	Thos. Byrne, Leather Goods, 50 Water Street
New Castle, Pa.	Emery Studio, Gift Shop. 13 N. Mill
New Haven, Conn.	Shartenberg & Robinson Co., Department Store
New London, Conn.	F. C. Chidsey, Stationery
New Orleans	F. F. Hansell & Bros.
New Rochelle, N. Y.	Pollyanna Gift Shop
New York City	Ovington's, 436-438 Fifth Avenue
Niagara Falls, N. Y.	E. M. Wittigschlager, Jeweler, 30 Falls Street
Northampton, Mass.	Hampshire Book Shop, 192 Main Street
North Platte, Neb.	Harry Dixon, Jeweler

Original, striking, beautiful! are the Hand-made things in Copper and Leather made by the Roycrofters. They are on sale in the Roycroft Shop in your town. See them!

North Yakima, Wash.	The Bon Ami, China, Glassware, Art Goods
Norwalk, Ohio	C. S. Bateham, Photo Supply & Art Goods
Oakland, Calif.	Fred N. Morcom, Art Goods, 1445 Broadway
Oberlin, Ohio	A. G. Comings & Son, Books, 37 W. College Street
Oil City, Pa.	R. G. Koch & Co.
Olean, N. Y.	Chas. W. Kulp, Art Goods, 141 N. Union
Omaha, Neb.	Orchard & Wilhelm Co., Home Furnishings
Ontario, Calif.	Rumel's Books & Stationery
Oswego, N. Y.	John M. Schuler & Son, Books & Art Goods
Ottawa, Ill.	F. S. Keeler & Co., Jewelers
Owego, N. Y.	W. H. Corey, Jr.
Owensboro, Ky.	Gant's Book Store
Oxford,Ohio	Snyder Art & Gift Shop
Palm Beach, Florida	C. R. Bennett Co.
Palo Alto, Calif.	Berton W. Crandall, Photo Supplies, 124 University Ave.
Parkersburg, W. Va.	J. W. Mather & Son, Jewelers, Market & 6th
Parsons, Kans.	M. F. Kohler, Jeweler, 1822 Main
Pasadena, Calif.	Herbert F. Brown, Books & Stationery
Paterson, N. J.	Wolfhegel & Co., Jewelers, 175 Market
Peekskill, N. Y.	C. S. Acker
Pensacola, Fla.	Rox Stationery & Gift Shop
Pendleton, Ore.	Frazier Book Store
Penn Yan, N. Y.	The Print Craft Shop
Perth Amboy, N. J.	Benham Art Shop
Petaluma, Calif.	Geo. H. Ott, Stationery & Gift Shop
Philadelphia, Pa.	Houston Club Book Store
Philadelphia, Pa.	Miss Wolcotts Gift Shop
Phoenix, Arizona	Miller-Sterling Co., Stationery, Books, Art Goods
Pinehurst. N. C.	Clow's Gift Shop
Pittsburgh	Jos. Horne Co., Department Store
Pittsfield, Mass.	The Meyer Store
Plainfield, N. J.	Tepper Brothers
Pomona, Calif.	Frashers, Books & Stationery
Portland, Ore.	M. L. Smith, Heilig Theatre Building, Jeweler
Porterville, Calif.	Hardell's Book Store
Poughkeepsie, N. Y.	Poughkeepsie Flag Shop
Prescott, Arizona	O. A. Hesla Co., Jewelers
Providence, R. I.	Tilden-Thurber Co , Jewelers
Pueblo, Colo.	Broome Bros. Books & Stationery
Pullman, Wash.	Student's Book Co.
Racine, Wisc.	The Treasure Chest
Reading, Pa.	C. K. Whitner & Co., Dept. Store
Redlands, Calif.	The Art Shop, Max F. Cunningham
Richmond, Ind.	Jenkins & Co., Jewelers
Richmond, Va.	Everett Waddey Co., Stationers, 1105 E. Main
Riverside, Calif.	F. W. Twogood, Photo Supply Shop, 700 Main Stree
Rochester, N. Y.	Marks & Fuller, Art Goods
Rochester, N. Y.	Scrantom's, Booksellers
Rockford, Ill.	Louise D. Hill, Art Shop
Roseburg, Ore.	Bryan's Gift Shop
Rutland, Vt.	Charles Stearns & Co.
Salamanca, N. Y.	E. F. Norton Co. Inc., Jewelers
Sacramento, Calif.	John Breuner Co., 604 K Street
Sacramento, Calif.	Hale Bros. Inc., Department Store
Salem, Ohio	McMillan's Book Shop
Salem, Oregon	Commercial Book Store
Salinas, Calif.	Mrs. Jessie M. Hughes, Stationery
Salt Lake City	Keith-O'Brien Co., Department Store
San Antonio, Texas	E. Hertzberg Jewelry Co., Houston & St. Mary's Sts.
San Bernardino, Calif.	Barnum-Flagg Co.
San Diego, Calif.	J. Jessop & Sons, Inc., Jewelers, Stationers
San Francisco	Paul Elder & Co., Booksellers, Grant Avenue
San Francisco	Adeline C. Bates, Book Shop, 1591 Haight Street
San Francisco	The Emporium, Department Store
San Jose, Calif.	G. J. Denne, Art Goods, 40 So. Second Street
San Mateo, Calif.	H. A. Clark, Stationery & Art Store

Mebbe our new illustrated Catalog listing Roycroft Hand-made things will help you in the selection of your Christmas gifts. Certainly we'll mail it to you if you say the word.

San Rafael, Calif.	J. D. Bennett, Jeweler
Santa Ana, Calif.	Santa Ana Book Store, 105 4th Street
Santa Barbara, Calif.	W. W. Osborne, Books & Stationery
Santa Cruz, Calif.	Fred R. Howe, Stationery & Musical Instruments
Santa Monica, Calif.	Byshe & Sons, Art Shop
Santa Rita, N. M.	Santa Rita Store Co.
Santa Rosa, Calif.	C. M. Bruner, Art Goods, 426 Fourth Street
Schenectady, N. Y.	Sterling Art Shop, 212 State Street
Scranton, Pa,	H. G, Dale Sons & Co.
Seattle, Wash.	Frederick & Nelson, Department Store
Seattle, Wash.	Linholm Book Store, 4344 14th Ave. N. E.
Sharon, Pa.	Frank G. Wengler, Jeweler, 306 E. State
Scheboygan, Wise,	The Art Shop
Sioux City, Iowa	The Pelletier Co., Home Furnishers
Silver City, N. Mexico	Mrs. Gilliland's Gift Shop
South Bend, Ind.	Makielski Art Ship
Spokane, Wash.	Culbertson Department Store
Springfield, Ill.	Coe Bros., Stationery, Photo Supplies, 5th & Monroe
Springfield, Ohio	The Buntell-Roth Co., 25 S. Fountain Avenue
Springfield, Mass.	Johnson's Book Store, 391 Main Street
State College, Pa.	L. K. Metzger
St. Joseph, Mich	Edith K. Allen, Gift Shop
St. Louis	Stix, Baer & Fuller, Department Store
St. Paul, Minn.	The Golden Rule Department Store
Steubenville, Ohio	Palmer Gift Shoppe
Stockton, Calif.	Blanche Angell
Streator, Ill.	W. H. Carew, Jeweler
Sunbury, Pa.	Rippel Art Shop, 356 Market Street
Syracuse, N. Y.	Dey Bros. & Co., Department Store
Tacoma, Wash.	Holt Art Store, 904 Commerce Street
Tampa, Fla,	Knight & Wall Co,
Titusville, Pa.	Ropp-Schreve Decorative Co.
Toledo, Ohio	LaSalle & Koch Co,
Topeka, Kans.	C. A. Wolf, Jeweler
Topeka, Kans.	Vaughn Smith Drug Co.
Toronto, Ont. Can.	Ellis Bros., Jewelers, 98 Yonge Street
Trenton, N. J.	A. V. Manning's Sons
Tuscon, Ariz,	Greenwald & Adams
Utica, N. Y.	Utica Office Supply Co,
Uhrichsville, Ohio	P. G. Lanning & Sons
Ventura, Calif.	MacGregor Bros.
Vicksburg, Miss.	Robert Ernst, Jewelry, 1306 Washington Street
Walla Walla, Wash.	Chapelle's Gift Shop
Waltham, Mass.	A. S. Ball, Stationery
Warren, Ohio	Colonel McFarland, Art Goods, Store Block
Warren, Pa.	Metzger-Wright Co.
Washington, D. C.	Woodward & Lothrop, Department Store
Waterbury, Conn.	Curtis Art Co., 25 W. Main Street
Waterloo, Iowa	W. T. Warwick, Books and Stationery
Wayluku, Hawaii	Maui Book Store, H. M. Linton, Prop.
Wellesley, Mass.	Sue Rice Art Shop
Wellsboro, Pa.	Frank Pagan, Jeweler
Westfield, N. Y.	G. L. Thomas
Wheeling, W. Va.	Sydney R. McCoy, Art Store
White Sulphur Springs, W. Va.	Foster & Reynolds Co., Remembrance Shop
Wilkes-Barre, Pa.	MacWilliams Co.
Williamsport, Pa.	Bert Wood Gift Shop
Wilmington, Del.	Geo. Hardcastle & Son, Art Goods, 417 Shipley
Winfield, Kans.	E. H. Pierce, Books & Stationery
Winona, Minn.	Allyn S. Morgan, Jeweler
Woodland, Calif.	J. T. Lawrence, Stationery
Wooster, Ohio	City Book Store
Worcester, Mass.	Robert E. Wesson Jr.
York, Pa.	The Regal Co.
Youngstown, Ohio	G. M. McKelvey, Department Store
Zanesville, Ohio	Ohio Office Supply Co.

*If there is no Roycroft Shop in your town send for our new illustrated Catalog
of Hand-made things that make dandy gifts.*

turned if they didn't sell to the public. So they ultimately had to be sold where they were, and, of course, they were sold. So, today, in virtually every major city there is a potentially large, scattered cache of worthy collectors' items. Today's collector, armed with an early Roycroft advertising list of stores that once had a Roycroft Department, has a pretty good idea as to where Roycroft items are likely to be found—in the attics, storage houses, antique shops, yard and garage sales, and flea markets of the particular cities listed.

What to look for in copper, brass, and silver? It is well nigh impossible to compile an accurate, fully descriptive listing of each and every item manufactured in the ever-changing variety that marked the amazing creativity of the Roycrofters over so many years. However, *all* are worth collecting and all worth collecting have the distinctive Roycroft trademark or the name, Roycroft, accompanied by the symbol, prominently stamped on them.

For the most part, Roycroft wares in any of the metals were hammered or etched. Very few had a completely smooth surface. Additionally, Roycroft wares in the main utilized heavy gauge copper and brass. Few, indeed, were thin and light. One develops a "feel" for Roycroft, in addition to the other unmistakable identifying characteristics.

For a broad idea of the kinds of copper, brass, and silver items to look for in Roycroft, here are some of the objects:

Vases (large and small), lamps, desk sets (ink wells, pen trays, stamp boxes, blotter holders, desk pads, stationery racks), bookends, bonbon boxes, nut bowls, nut plates, nut service spoons and picks, bowls of many sizes and shapes, including finger bowls and bowls for jardinieres and ferneries, bud vases, trays of all sizes and shapes for a variety of common uses, smokers' sets (ash trays, matchbox holders, pipe racks, cigarette boxes and cups and humidors), desk calendars, free-standing picture frames, candlesticks, sconces and candleabra, pot holders, door knockers, paper knives, tea bells, memo pad holders, incense burners, napkin rings, jewelry (hat pins, bracelets, cuff links, etc.)

This is not an all-inclusive list. It covers the basic categories and demonstrates the collector potential which is further enlarged by the wide variety of designs and finishes that took place in all of these from year to year.

It will become more and more evident further along in this guide to Roycroft collecting that Hubbard/Roycroft buffs gather in anything and everything related to the subject. However, without question, the greatest activity—and the greatest potential for collectors and dealers insofar as available quantity and monetary values are concerned—lies, thus far, in the collection of the books and the brass, copper, and silver items.

Terra Cotta and Pottery

Sculpture was never one of the large-scale arts and crafts at the Roycroft, nor was the making of pottery. However enough of each was done there as to make the finding of examples of it still possible today, however remote the possibility may be.

A rare 1899 catalog from the Roycroft, titled *A Few Bits Of Sculpture In Terra Cotta As Made By Saint Gerome At The Roycroft Shop, East Aurora, New York, U.S.A.,* carries photos of eight examples of the work of Jerome Conner that were offered for sale. Included were bas reliefs of Elbert Hubbard, Richard Wagner, Walt Whitman, and Katherine (a daughter of Elbert Hubbard). Also busts, titled, *Japanese Girl, Ruth, Fra Elbertus* (Hubbard), and *Hamlet.* The catalog does not indicate whether or not more than one of each was available, though it does not seem likely that there were. (*Japanese Girl* survived and is in this author's private collection. Walt Whitman is in a private collection as may be some of the others.)

Payroll records of the Roycroft indicate that a "Miss Douglass" worked in 1900 in pottery, but there is no indication that any substantial pottery output and sales were reached. Roycroft designer, Dard Hunter, made several pieces of pottery with the Roycroft trademark on them, but the only known pieces extant are in the possession of Dard Hunter, Jr. The only other pottery found occasionally today bearing the Roycroft trademark are brown jugs, jars, and cups made for them which were sold on the Campus filled with maple syrup, candy, and shaving soap, respectively. (Some of the jars thus far located are also in blue and rose.)

A FEW BITS OF SCULPTURE IN TERRA COTTA AS MADE BY SAINT GEROME AT THE ROYCROFT SHOP EAST AURORA NEW YORK U.S.A.

Sculpture

Made from genuine East Aurora clay as dug by Ali Baba from the bank by the dam-side, and modeled by Saint Gerome in an Idle Hour:

BUST, in terra cotta, of Fra
 Elbertus, $5.00
 Three-quarters life size.

BAS RELIEF of Franz Liszt   3.00
 Panel shape, 7x10.

BAS RELIEF of Walt Whit-
 man,   3.00
 Round, 9 inches in diameter.

BAS RELIEF—" Gladys,"   2.00
 Panel, 6x8.

PAPER WEIGHT—Roycroft   .50

THE ROYCROFTERS
East Aurora
N. Y.

Sculptured pieces in terra cotta, done by Jerome Conner ("Saint Gerome") were offered briefly by the Roycrofter in 1899. A small catalog was issued and only for that one year. It is a rare item.

Hooked Rugs

In the *Philistine* magazine the Roycrofters advertised hooked rugs "made by the girls at the Roycroft." If marked Roycroft and found today they would be of interest to the complete Roycroft collector, but none are known to be still in existence.

R AG CARPETS—The Old Fashioned kind. Woven roycroftie— stout, durable, beautiful—in East Aurora by Roycroft girls (seventy years young). Rugs in three yard lengths, price Three Dollars, or in quantities One Dollar a yard. Address THE ROYCROFT SHOP, East Aurora, New York.

Hard to find today with sewed-on cloth Roycroft labels, but something to look for!

Other Products

Hardly falling into the pure crafts category, but certainly related collectors' items, are the non-Roycroft-made, but Roycroft-marked cardboard candy cartons, the aforementioned jugs, jars, and cups utilized in making up gift packages of Roycroft farm and candy kitchen products. These were sold in the Roycroft Campus store, along with other Roycroft products, and via mail order. The full assortment of edibles were packaged in mahogany "Goody Boxes" made in the Roycroft Furniture Shop. They were 12½″ × 23″ × 9½″ deep and handsomely adorned with hammered copper side handles, hinges, and hasp. The Roycroft trademark was carved on the lid.

Roycrofters Who Added Dimensions to Roycroft Collecting

All of the hundreds of employees of the Roycroft, whatever their job, made their contributions to the success of that unique crafts complex which left such a vast legacy to today's collectors. But there were several whose personal attributes and reputations added an extra dimension which markedly affects today's collecting of direct and associated Roycroft items.

Several, but not necessarily all of them, are discussed here for the guidance of Roycroft collectors. Most of the key such figures were wooed to the Roycroft by Elbert Hubbard, himself, and during the time that he directed the enterprises.

Where are they today?
They're part of the complete Roycroft collectors' search.

ROYCROFT
WHITE CLOVER HONEY
in an OLD FASHIONED BROWN CROCK

With a little brown lid, properly corked and hermetically sealed with red sealing wax. The quantity is 14 ounces.

When empty this crock will hold sufficient Boston Baked Beans for two and makes a charming decoration for any Luncheon Table!

There's a Recipe Book for uses of Honey tied to this crock with a silken cord.

Price $1.35

THE ROYCROFTERS, EAST AURORA, N.Y.

Roycroft Maple Syrup and Maple Pecan Patties

MAPLE sugar making is " free and fascinating, half work and half play," said Ol' John Burroughs.

Every man who once " helped 'round " in a sugar camp carries forever the memory of the woods, the fragrant smell of the boiling sap, and the rich taste of the syrup.

At the Roycroft sugar-bush, printers, craftsmen, writers and artists hustle in the woods by day to make the rounds and collect the sap, and all night while the moon rides high they pile in the fuel and boil the sap down to its richest essence.

(To make one quart of Roycroft Maple Syrup it takes thirty-three quarts of Maple Sap boiled down (over a wood fire).

(Every year we use hundreds of gallons of Maple Syrup to make the famous Roycroft Pecan Patties, a soft delicious confection made and shipped fresh every day. And the first run syrup this year is the best ever! Roycroft Maple Syrup is shipped in tightly sealed quart cans. Our Syrup is not to be confused with the commercial product found in the city markets. It is the richest and most delicious first-run syrup you ever tasted.

The quart cans contain one quart plus, or three pounds, net, and are priced at $1.25 postpaid east of the Mississippi River, and $1.50 postpaid west of the Mississippi.

USE THIS COUPON

- -

THE ROYCROFTERS, EAST AURORA, N.Y.

Please send me ....cartons of one dozen Patties each at - - $ .90

............cartons of two dozen Patties each at - - 1.70

............quarts of Pure 1926 first-run Maple Syrup 1.25

............quarts delivered West of Mississippi River 1.50

The above price to include transportation charges

Your Name..

Date............ Address..

Roycroft maple syrup cans with the labels still affixed have become collectibles, along with Roycroft pecan patties boxes.

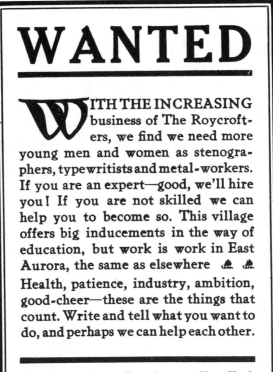

WANTED

WITH THE INCREASING business of The Roycrofters, we find we need more young men and women as stenographers, typewritists and metal-workers. If you are an expert—good, we'll hire you! If you are not skilled we can help you to become so. This village offers big inducements in the way of education, but work is work in East Aurora, the same as elsewhere ♣ ♣ Health, patience, industry, ambition, good-cheer—these are the things that count. Write and tell what you want to do, and perhaps we can help each other.

The Roycrofters, East Aurora, New York

Hubbard's opinion writings in the Philistine *magazine attracted the avant garde and, while he had their attention, he lured many to come and work for him through ads like this in the publication.*

Roycroft sculptor, Jerome Conner, fashioned this bust of Elbert Hubbard in terra cotta in 1899.

(Some came later, influenced by his lingering inspiration and the influence of Elbert Hubbard II who kept the operation afloat for another twenty-three years after the untimely death of his father in 1915. Those Roycrofters will be touched upon in chapter 3 of this book.)

Sculptor

Sculptor Jerome Conner, previously mentioned, came to the Roycroft in 1898 and subsequently went on to become recognized in his own right as an independent and successful sculptor. Many years later he was commissioned by Elbert Hubbard II to come back and do the heroic size bronze statue of Hubbard that still stands in East Aurora. His works, whether done during his Roycroft days or later, are considered to be exceptionally worthy collectors' items.

Artists

Artist W. W. Denslow was lured by Hubbard in 1897 to come to the Roycroft to teach local girls the art of hand-illumining. He created the seahorse Roycroft watermark design that adorned the imported handmade paper used in the earliest Roycroft books, and, himself, ornamented and/or designed the ornamentations for those early books. He left the Roycroft around 1907 and gained lasting individual fame as the illustrator of the *Wizard of Oz.* Today there are Denslow collectors and his later fame now enhances the value of any Roycroft items identifiable to him.

Artist-Designer-Craftsman Dard Hunter well earned those titles in the atelier atmosphere of the Roycroft where he was lured in 1903, at the age of 20, purely and simply by the intriguing sound of the place as colorfully portrayed in the *Philistine* magazine to which his older brother subscribed.

He was a student at Ohio State University where he had examined books made at the Kelmscott Press of William Morris. Coming from a long line of Ohio newspaper publishers, he already had printer's ink in his blood. With summer vacation coming up, he wrote to Hubbard seeking a summer job at the place that seemed akin to the Kelmscott. As he later explained in his autobiography, *My Life With Paper,* Hubbard was not particularly encouraging but not sufficiently discouraging to keep him from taking the train to East Aurora.

He was hired and soon sent away by Hubbard to work in the stained glass studio of J. and R. Lamb, architects of church interiors, in New York City. He came back in a few weeks a sufficiently trained craftsman to do the leaded-glass windows that still grace the Roycroft, and to ultimately turn out the magnificent stained-glass hallway chandelier that still hangs, plus a considerable number of

ALI BABA

Book plate design by W. W. Denslow who went on to greater fame as an illustrator after he left the Roycroft.

leaded-glass Roycroft table lamps that bring hundreds of dollars today, largely because they were Dard Hunter pieces.

Hunter designed the cover page of the *FRA* magazine and dozens of Roycroft pamphlets. He designed the title pages of the "Little Journeys to the Homes of Great Businessmen" in that magazine series, and numerous Roycroft book title pages. His distinctive, more modern art is easily recognized over that of other Roycroft designer-artists even before examining it closely for the generally present "DH" initials, with the D reversed.

Any Roycroft printed matter of established collector price today automatically gains at least a fifty percent increase if it is one of Dard Hunter design on the cover or title page.

Hunter stayed several years at the Roycroft and went on to become recognized as one of the world's leading authorities on paper making. He ultimately came to make his own handmade paper, design his own type, and produce his own limited-edition books, some of which sell for thousands of dollars today.

Artist Burt Barnes who had been a successful commercial artist

Book plate design by Dard Hunter who, after his Roycroft days went on to become heralded as a world authority on papermaking.

WORK your Grief up into ART and it is GONE

Motto design by artist Burt Barnes whose pre- and post-Roycroft art, along with the work he did there, is just now gaining national acclaim.

No.		Each illum.	Each plain
216	We thank Thee for this place in which we dwell, for the love that unites, etc.	$	.25 / .10
217	What others say of me matters little; what I myself say and do matters much		.25
218	What would be the good of havin' luck if nobody was glad; or of gettin' things if there was nobody to divide with?		.15
219	Whenever any good comes our way, let us enjoy it to the fullest and then pass it along in another form		.25
220	Whenever you go out-of-doors, draw your chin in, carry the crown of the head high, etc.	1.00	.25
221	When you disparage the concern of which you are a part, you disparage yourself		.25
222	White Hyacinths: If I had but two loaves of bread, etc.		.25
223	Who entereth here?	1.00	.25
224	Why not leave them to Nemesis?	.15	.10
225	Worry, hate and unkindness are all forms of fear		.25
226	Work for yourself by working for the good of all		.25
227	Yesterday can not be recalled; tomorrow can not be assured; this day only is yours		.25
228	You can never stand well with the boss by telling him of those who are laggards		.25
229	You have not fulfilled every duty unless you have fulfilled that of being pleasant	1.00	.25
230	Your heart does the work		.25
231	Your quarrel with the world is only a quarrel with yourself		.25

Hubbard fans could buy his pithy mottoes on cards especially designed by Roycroft artists. They're collectibles today. This is a descriptive price list page from the Motto Book, a catalog of such.

and illustrator in Chicago, had received some formal training at the Chicago Art Institute and had exhibited there, joined the Roycrofters in 1908. He remained only a year and a half but long enough to have his efforts included in Roycroft magazines, books, and motto cards.

After leaving the Roycroft he worked in relative obscurity for the remainder of his life but many of his works, before, during, and after his Roycroft period are today reassessed and more appreciated. There was an exhibition of his work at the University Art Museum, University of New Mexico, in 1974. Information about him and his work is now in the microfilm library of the Archives of American Art, an affiliate of the Smithsonian Institution. His star seems to be rising, long after his death and his one-time association with the Roycrofters. This will certainly enhance the value of Barnes-illustrated Roycroft books and printings, most of which carry the "BB" initials as a signature.

There are Roycroft collectors who seek examples of the work of such other *artist-illustrator-designers, Carl Ahrens, Mazzanovich, Samuel Warner, Otto Schneider, Jules Gaspard, Raymond Nott, Albert Miller, Emil and Axel Sahlin, Lillian Bonham* and others of this Roycroft heyday period.

Warner was the first Roycroft artist. Gaspard and Schneider and Nott were above average in portraiture. Nott and Miller were good

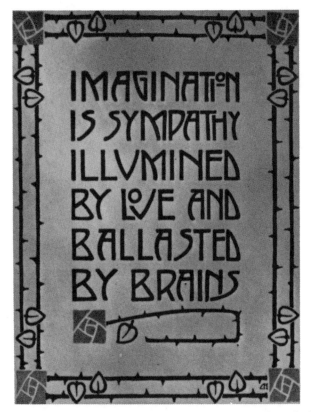

An example of Dard Hunter's design work for motto cards and placards.

80

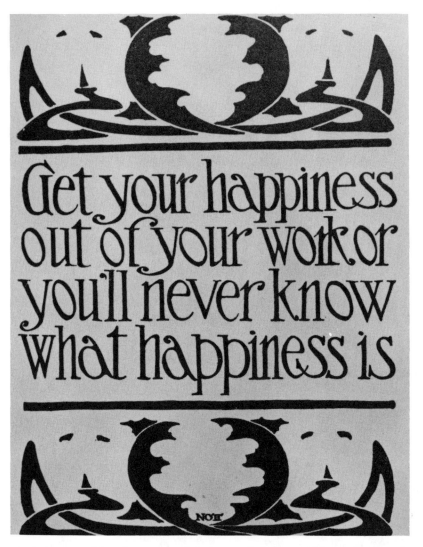

Artist Raymond Nott's motto card design work showcased his particular style.

at caricatures while Gaspard and Schneider drew the fine likenesses of the many famous persons that Hubbard drew word pictures of in his "Little Journeys" biographical sketches or featured in the *FRA* magazine. The latter two did many of these for FRA covers. More and more pieces of the original art of all these Roycroft artists are coming to the surface today and have high price tags on them.

Two Roycroft artists, recognized before and after their association with Hubbard as prominent oil painters in their own right, were *Alexis Fournier* and *Sandor Landeau*.

Fournier came to the Roycroft in 1903, being lured there by Hubbard through correspondence in 1902. He remained with the Roycrofters longer than any of the artists, nearly to the very end of the enterprises in the late 1930s, and spent the remainder of his life in East Aurora. The murals that Hubbard commissioned him to do for the salon of the Roycroft Inn are great works of art that remain in the landmark edifice today. Others of his many oils are owned by

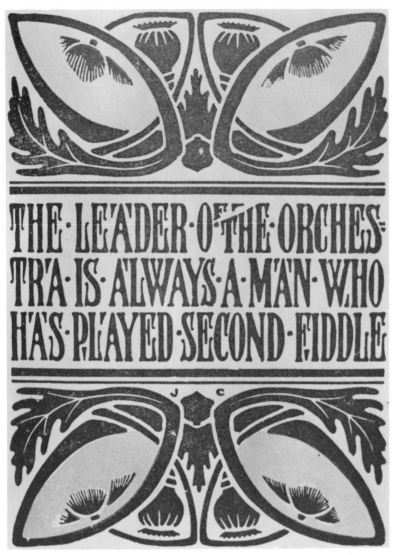

Even sculptor Jerome Conner tried his hand at decorating motto cards!

Artist Samuel Warner whose pen and ink sketches of famous persons for Hubbard's Little Journeys *magazine designed Hubbard's first book plate.*

An example of the art of Otto Schneider, a contemporary of Jules Gaspard and Dard Hunter at the Roycroft.

The portraiture of Jules Maurice Gaspard who was one of the better trained, better known artists to become art director of the Roycroft.

the Aurora Historical Society, Inc. and private collectors. As the interest in collecting Roycroft and associated items grows, more and more Fournier paintings are coming out of attics and estates and being sold. Some are now valued in the thousands.

Landeau was more of an artist-in-residence at the Roycroft for the relatively short period (one or two years) that he was a part of the organization. He arrived in 1915, bringing with him many of the paintings for which he had been accorded significant honors. The idea, it seems, was that he would be available to do commissioned work for any of the desiring prominent persons who were by then coming to the Inn to meet Hubbard and soak up the arts and crafts atmosphere of the total complex.

Like Fournier, he had studied in the United States and Paris. He had lived in Paris for twenty-five years previous to coming back to

Artist Albert W. Miller was a specialist in cartoons which Hubbard liked to tip-in or use as back cover art for the Philistine *magazine. His work, too, is collected today but mostly for its connection with Roycroft collectibles.*

America and making this connection with the Roycrofters. At Paris, Landeau had studied under Jean Paul Laurens and Benjamin Constant. He received a Gold Medal for his painting, *Prayer for Lost Seamen* in a Paris Salon in 1907. He had traveled and painted extensively in Europe including Russia, in Egypt, the Holy Land, Morocco, Mexico, and the United States. Fifty of his paintings were exhibited at the Broderick Galleries in Buffalo in 1916 and some were offered for sale. The price tag on the *Lost Seamen* was $20,000 but it wasn't sold. That painting is now owned by the Aurora Historical Society. Others were acquired by Elbert Hubbard and little is known about where these and others of his works are today. The search for Landeau paintings has become a facet of Roycroft

ALEXIS FOURNIER,
Art Director.

Roycroft artists Alexis Fournier, by Fournier. He succeeded Gaspard as art director.

collecting . . . and the rewards become increasingly worthwhile.

Hubbard "discovered" numerous artists and his lingering influence on Hubbard/Roycroft devotees is bringing about their re-discovery today.

Metal Craftsmen

It is said that there was never a really sloppy craftsman working in the trade in the Roycroft Copper Shop and examination of their output (other than the first two items offered for sale) gives credence to the statement.

Individual craftsmen did not affix a personal mark, just the official Roycroft trademark, and so it is not easy to single out the work of every individual. However, several of them eventually operated shops of their own, either in a building of their own for that purpose or a room of their home, after leaving Hubbard's employ. Examples of their work, bearing their own marks, are Roycroft-associated collectors' items today and often bring as much—and sometimes more—than Roycroft pieces.

Examples of the craftsmanship of Walter U. Jennings in his post-Roycroft days. He learned metalcrafting at the Roycroft. Collecting the later Jennings' pieces is today an extension of Roycroft collecting. They are superb in design and craftsmanship.

Among these, the more easily recognized are the pieces done by *Karl Kipp, Walter U. Jennings,* and *Arthur Cole* because those craftsmen followed the pursuit nearly fulltime after leaving the Roycroft. But also quite talented and well-known were *Henry Unverdorf, Roy Johnson,* and *Leon Varley* who continued their crafts work but along with other pursuits.

Karl Kipp came to the Roycroft in 1908 and with Hubbard's encouragement became the person to build the copper craftsmen into a cohesive and highly creative group in 1909. He was really the father of the Roycroft Copper Shop. He headed it while Hubbard lived, left for a time, and was beckoned back later in the same position by Elbert Hubbard II. When he was on his own he operated the TooKay Shop in East Aurora and even had a sales and display room in New York City for a short period of time. TooKay pieces are much-collected and treasured today.

The same is true of the signed Jennings pieces. Walter Jennings was another of those Roycrofters who were originally drawn to Hubbard's fold through the latter's magnetic rhetoric in the little *Philistine* magazine. Prior to a chance reading of the *Phil* at a bookshop at Troy, New York in 1906, Jennings had been a reasonably contented superintendent of a knitting mill in that Upstate New York industrial city. But he was soon hooked by the Roycroft mystique and by 1908 yielded to the call. That year he gave up his good position to accept one of much less importance in the bindery of the Roycroft Print Shop, bringing a wife and three young children to being life anew in East Aurora.

A fellow new employee, then also of the bindery, was Karl Kipp who, the next year, took Jennings with him into the Copper Shop he had been assigned by Hubbard to take over and build. Later, when Kipp left the Roycroft the first time, Jennings went with him to the TooKay Shop. But he returned to the Roycroft when Kipp did and remained there until 1933, when he went to work for the Avon Coppersmith at Avon, New York until the early 1940s when he established his own shop in East Aurora.

Arthur Cole was a fellow craftsman with Kipp and Jennings but did not linger as long as they at the Roycroft. He established the highly successful Avon Coppersmith shop at Avon where Jennings worked for a time in the mid-1930s. Cole passed away recently but the enterprise he established still survives.

Bookbinders and Leather Modelers

The best known among the early Roycroft bookbinders and experts in the modeling of leather were, without a doubt, *Louis H. Kinder, Charles W. Youngers, Frederick Kranz, Lorenz Schwartz, Peter Franck, Sterling Lord,* and *George ScheideMantel.*

Kinder was the first expert bookbinder in Hubbard's employ.

Roycroft leather modeler Lorenz Schwartz drew this design for Hubbard's book, Hollyhocks and Goldenglow, executing then in full levant with hand tools for a special edition. His original drawings in pen and ink, such as this, are sought and treasured today.

Said to have been trained in Liepsig, he trained many of the others who came to work in the trade at the Roycroft. One of his prize pupils was Charles Youngers who later headed the bindery himself and ultimately became an officer of the company when the Roycrofters were incorporated. Both Youngers and Franck, in later years, bound some of Dard Hunter's early books on paper-making which are so valuable today.

Sterling Lord, who was also a contemporary of Hunter's at the

Expert leather modeler Frederick (Fritz) Kranz also tried his hand at lamp designing. This rare original pencil sketch is in the author's collection.

Roycroft, was, by 1910 following the bookbinding craft in London in the employ of the respected old Zaehnsdorf Bookbindery.

George ScheideMantel joined the Roycroft as a bellhop at the Roycroft in 1905, remained only a year, and left to get a better paying clerk's job in Buffalo so he could marry Gladys Grant, daughter of Mother Grant, the head cook at the Roycroft Inn.

Meanwhile, wanting to be a Roycrofter, he went to work in 1913 for Frederick Kranz who by then had also left Hubbard's employ and had formed his own Cordova Shops, specializing in fine modeled leather goods. By 1915, ScheideMantel had learned the craft so well under Kranz's tutelage that he was offered the top position in the Roycroft Leather Shop. He headed it from 1915 until 1918 when he opened a design studio of his own in leather art and bookbinding.

In many, but not all instances, the works of these craftsmen are today identifiable by signatures or, in some Roycroft books, through credits carried in the colophons.

Writers

Very few writers at the Roycroft received by-lines. Among the anonymous were *Walter Blackburn Harte, Michael Monahan,* and *Sadakichi Hartman.* However, these men all came to be known through media vehicles of their own, and because they were once bona fide Roycrofters, collectors add these other items to their Roycroft collections as association items.

Walter Blackburn Harte of Boston advertised his Fly Leaf *magazine in the March 1896 issue of Hubbard's* Philistine *magazine. It competed in size and commentary with the "Phil." Hubbard promptly persuaded Harte to abandon publication of the* Fly Leaf. *The alliance was short-lived but the* Fly Leaf *was dead too. Because of the history, Harte's magazine has become a Roycroft-associated collector's item.*

Harte began publication of *The Fly Leaf* in December, 1895, at Boston, Massachusetts. It was much like Hubbard's *Philistine* in format. In 1896, Hubbard persuaded Harte to give up his magazine and to join him in the publication of the *Philistine*. The association lasted about a month. The early issues of the *Fly Leaf* have thus become collectors' items.

Michael Monahan started a similar pocket-size magazine in 1903, *The Papyrus.* In due course he, too, went to work for Hubbard and also became disenchanted. Leaving, after a feud with Hubbard, he commenced publication of *The Phoenix* magazine. Both magazines, having "before" and "after" comments about Hubbard are significant to the complete Hubbard/Roycroft collector.

Sadakichi Hartmann, a Japanese-German poet, playwright, and art critic, was another on-campus writer who received no by-lines for his writings. But he authored several books of poems and histories on Japanese and American art which were published elsewhere and gained him recognition. He married Lillian Bonham, a Roycroft illustrator. Today there are Hartmann buffs and a nationally circulated *Sadakichi Hartmann Newsletter* for the exchange of information about him. His works are being revived. All such are these days being collected for their relationship to the Roycroft.

There were a few writers who spent brief periods as Roycrofters and *did* get by-lines, notably, *Charles (Carl) Sandburg* and *Richard Le Gallienne.*

As mentioned earlier, Stephen Crane's writings appeared in Hubbard's publications but as a contributor and not as an in-house writer.

Furniture Designers and Craftsmen

Herbert Buffum, Albert Danner, Tom Standeven, William Roth, James Cadzow, and *Victor Toothacker* were all listed as employees of the Roycroft Furniture Shop in its early days. All being skilled in woodworking, and being subjected to Hubbard's urgings to all Roycrofters to be innovative, it seems likely that they all came up with ideas for Roycroft furniture.

It is likely, too, that Cadzow and Roth, who came to be known as architects and builders in the village, made significant furniture design suggestions. However, the principal designer was, without a doubt, Victor Toothacker, whose furniture sketches in pen and ink (sometimes in a watercolor of a room setting) appeared in Roycroft furniture and other catalogs, along with his signature. But while the Roycroft trademark or the name, Roycroft, was carved prominently on the viewed surfaces of the furniture, no craftsman added his personal mark.

Some of Toothacker's original sketches have surfaced recently

Many of Hubbard's lectures were given advance publicity through postcards supplied by the Roycroft. Among the most treasured by collectors is this one. It touted what came to be his last lecture before his tragic death in the sinking of the S. S. Lusitania.

and are now in the possession of the Aurora Historical Society. Undoubtedly Roycroft collectors will be on the lookout for more of them. One of the watercolor sketches is in a private collection, having shown up at a flea market . . . and at a price said to have been between $50 and $100!

Other Hubbard/Roycroft Memorabilia

Elbert Hubbard's frank, imaginative, and sometimes pithy writing style endeared him to a wide cross section of readers. He had a wide following, from activists to world leaders, while he lived. And, because much of his comment is still apropos, he is being redis-covered and more appreciated today.

As a lecturer, he was very popular and was the highest paid one-man attraction on the Orpheum Circuit at the turn of the century. In addition, and unlike William Morris, he had an excep-tionally fertile mind for promotional ideas. These combined attrib-utes resulted in a large legacy of collectors' items which Hubbard/Roycroft devotees avidly seek today.

Among them were the little booklets he wrote about business firms and selected communities around the country. There are over 100 different ones to collect, plus, sometimes, variant editions of each with respect to covers, ornamentation, or size. Some of

THE SILO
AND WHICH ONE IS BEST

By
ELBERT HUBBARD

A 1910 Philistine *magazine ad urging firms and institutions to let Hubbard do advertising booklets for them. In-house they became known as the Business Little Journeys. He did over 100 of them and there are Roycroft collectors of these alone. Shown here are representative samples of the varying cover designs and range of titles. Those with covers by Dard Hunter are in greatest demand and bring best prices.*

The American National Assurance Company

BY

ELBERT HVBBARD

(FRA ELBERTVS)

THE ROYCROFTERS
EAST AVRORA ERIE COVNTY N.Y.

A LITTLE JOURNEY TO

UTAH

AND INVESTMENT OPPOR-TUNITIES I FOUND THERE

BY ELBERT HUBBARD

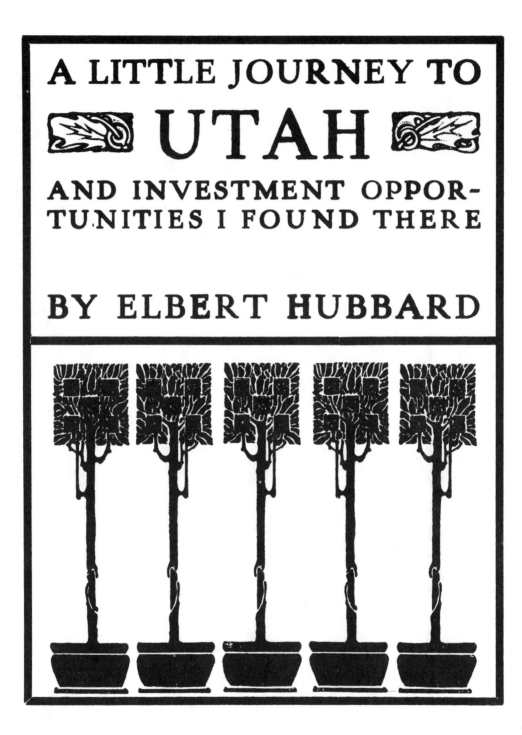

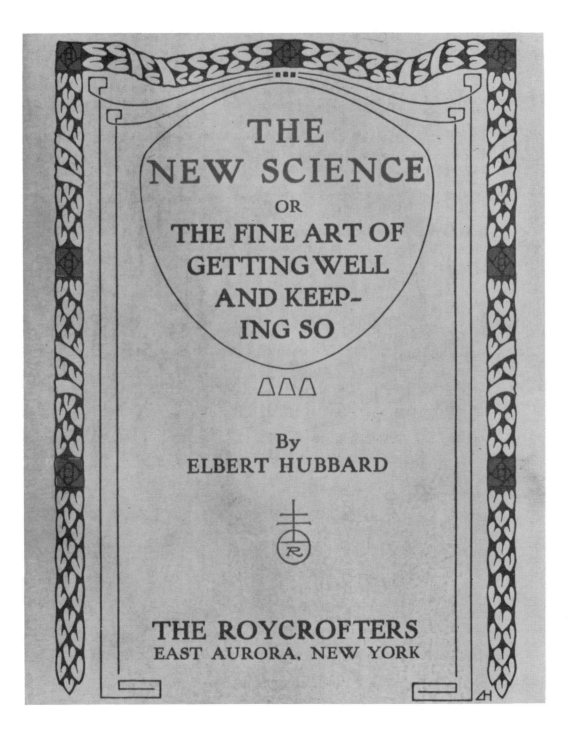

THE
NEW SCIENCE
OR
THE FINE ART OF
GETTING WELL
AND KEEP-
ING SO

△△△

By
ELBERT HUBBARD

THE ROYCROFTERS
EAST AURORA, NEW YORK

A Little Journey
to the Home of
JOHN ‑B‑
STETSON
by Elbert Hubbard

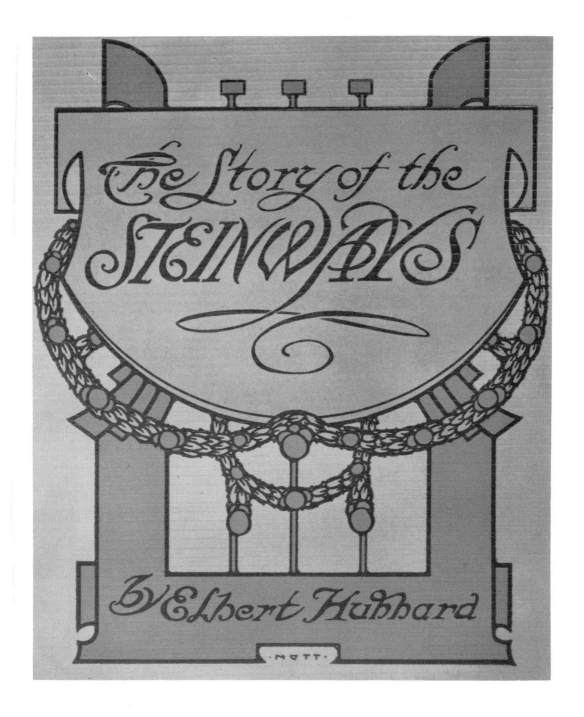

The Story of the STEINWAYS

by Elbert Hubbard

CASH &
FRIENDS

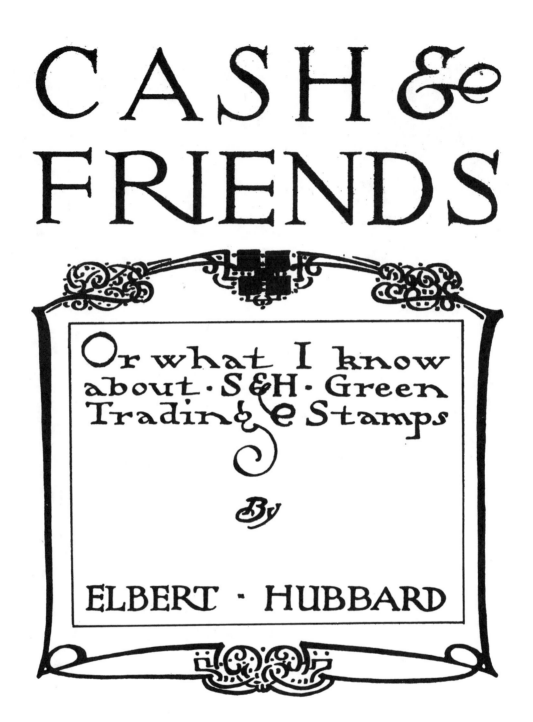

Or what I know
about · S&H · Green
Trading & Stamps

By

ELBERT · HUBBARD

these, for instance, are good examples of Dard Hunter's cover-design work.

Some collectors specialize in collecting different copies of his classic essay, *A Message to Garcia,* in different languages and the special cover imprint for firms and organizations who bought them for distribution to employees and friends. The *Message* was printed in eleven languages. Especially prized by collectors are the early reprints by the New York Central Railroad which really catapulted the message—and Hubbard—to lasting fame.

A prolific epigrammatist, Hubbard had the idea of printing them in postcard size, placard size (for framing), and even having them carved in wood plaques by the Roycroft Furniture Shop. He produced a catalog listing the various sayings available. Called *The Motto Book,* the catalog was updated from time to time and these, too, are collected today. Some mottoes are found today in Roycroft picture frames, as originally sold in some instances. Some are printed in color, some black and white, and some hand-illumined.

Some collectors specialize in gathering variant special issues of Hubbard's famous essay, A Message To Garcia. *Bought and distributed via mail or employer reading racks by the thousands, they are still around in relative abundance but early ones are sought by collectors.*

God must dearly
love the fools,
otherwise He would
not have made
so many of ~~all~~ them
—Elbert Hubbard

Postcard motto cards like this hold a special fascination for some Roycroft collectors today.

Full-color postcards (printed abroad) with scenes of the Roycroft Campus and/or photos of the Roycroft Inn and print shop interiors were sold by the thousands on the Campus. The same was true of cards bearing his photo and/or his epigrams. Unused or written on, they today sell to collectors for anywhere from $2 to $6 each!

Every weekend that Hubbard was in town he lectured in the Roycroft Salon. The audience was made up of Inn guests, Roycroft employees, and townspeople. The program also usually included a recital by Roycrofters or visiting talent singing, playing the piano or some other musical instrument. Most always, there was a printed program and there are collectors of these.

Year after year, hundreds of Hubbard fans came to Roycroft Conventions. Still existing programs, ribbons, canes, and other souvenirs from these events are collected today. The same is true of the many Roycroft advertising broadsides and Hubbard's printed poster messages to his employees that were taken from the bulletin boards and saved.

The Roycroft Print Shop specialized in personal bookplates, designed by Roycroft artists, for the general public. Some bore the initials of the artists (Warner, Nott, and others) and today are collected as examples of their work.

Roycroft and stamp collectors alike prize the Roycroft "perfins" —U.S. postage stamps perforated in the configuration of the Roycroft trademark for added promotional identification on mail sent out from that crafts complex.

A much-photographed man, Hubbard's portraits by some of the best known photographers of his day are collectors' items today. Actual reprints on photographic paper were brought in large

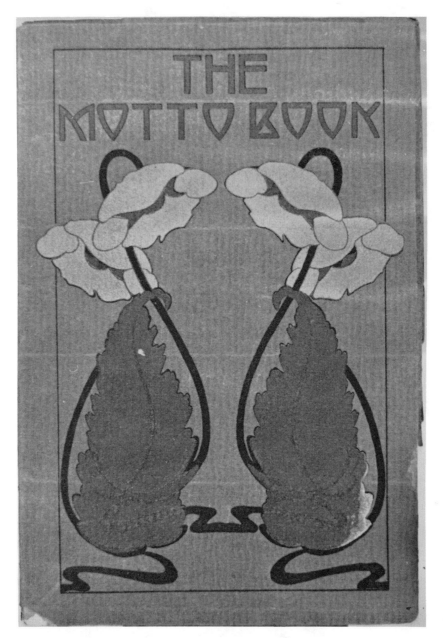

Collectors seek the Motto Book, a catalog of Roycroft mottos. This one, with a cover design by Dard Hunter, is a favorite among collectors.

quantities from the photographers and sold at the Roycroft to Hubbard fans. Some, of course, were given away, autographed. Some were given or sold in Roycroft frames making them a double value item today. There are such photos also of Alice Hubbard and of Alice and Elbert posing together.

Theater placards, tickets, postcards, and printed programs related to Hubbard's lecture appearances on the Orpheum Circuit all over the nation, including Carnegie Music Hall in New York City, were saved in each place by his fans and are being gathered up by collectors today. Rarer are similar mementos from Alice's brief

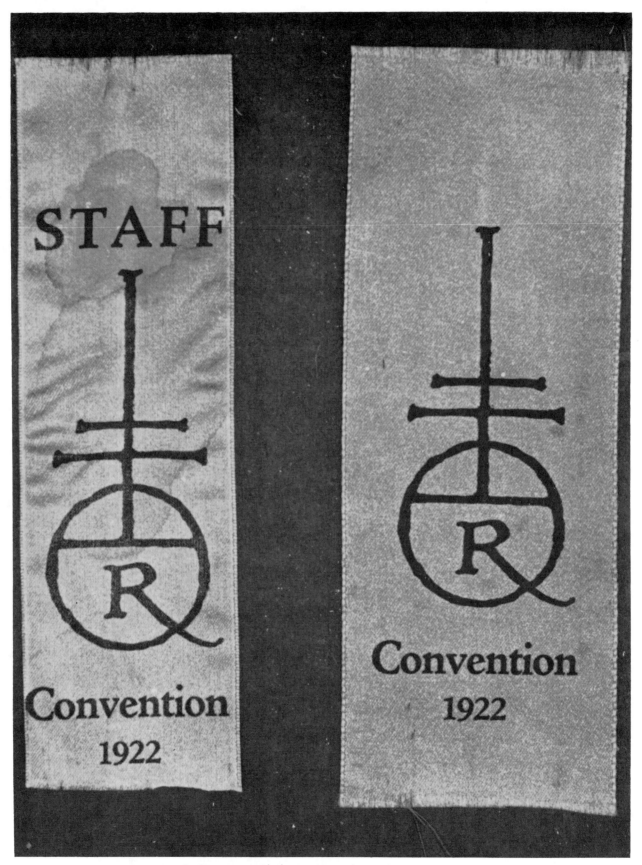

The goldenrod color silk ribbons for staff and visitors at the annual Roycroft conventions show up now and then and are quickly snapped up by collectors.

ROYCROFT CHAPEL

Sunday Evening, July XIII, MCMII

ORATORIO

A Ballade of the French Revolution,   *Chopin*
   R. R. von Liebich

Duet: "I would that my Love,"   *Mendelssohn*
   Miss Nettie Pratt and Mrs. Hubbard

Address: "Pericles,"
   Mr. Hubbard

Violin Solo: Serenade,   *Gounod*
   Donald Morrison

Address: "Is your Likeness your Own?"
   Mr. Sayles

Tannhauser-March (by request),   *Wagner-Liszt*
   R. R. von Liebich

Roycroft-printed programs for concerts and recitals held at the Roycroft Campus every week in Hubbard's day, plus programs from his appearances on the national lecture circuit are "musts" for the complete Roycroft collector. They are still around but not easy to find.

Stamp collectors and Roycroft buffs alike seek stamps that were pre-cancelled with the Roycroft trademark in the perforations.

East Aurora, N. Y._____ 191___

ELBERT HUBBARD, BANKER
(50-534)

Pay to the
Order of_____ $_____

_____ Dollars

No._____   _____

THE ROYCROFT SHOP

ELBERT HUBBARD
BANKING BUILDING

THE ROYCROFT CHAPEL

BUILT OF STONE—FIRE-PROOF. LARGE BURGLAR-PROOF VAULT AND SAFE.
SAFETY DEPOSIT BOXES FOR RENT.

Elbert Hubbard - Banker
ESTABLISHED 1903
East Aurora, N. Y.

1915		January			1915	
SUN.	MON.	TUE.	WED.	THU.	FRI.	SAT.
					1	2
3	4	5	6	7	8	9
10	11	12	13	14	15	16
17	18	19	20	21	22	23
24/31	25	26	27	28	29	30

Pays 4% Interest Per Annum, Compounded Quarterly

Hubbard's bank calendars and checks show up in antique shops now and then but are not there long if a Roycroft collector spots them. Hubbard was among the first, if not the very first, to promote the "bank by mail" concept.

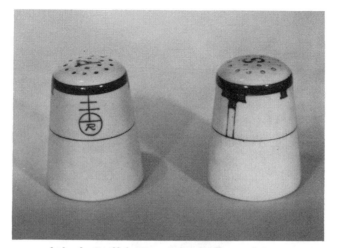

Salt and pepper set made by the Buffalo Pottery for the Roycroft Inn prominently displayed the Roycroft trademark. These, and other table-setting pieces by that pottery for the inn are today collected by both Roycroft and Buffalo Pottery buffs. As with all Buffalo Pottery today, the prices are quite high.

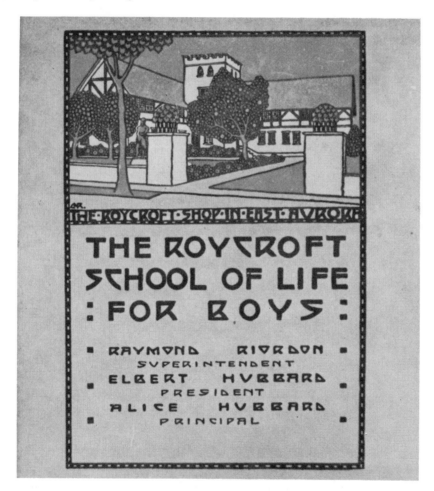

To attract and train young men to become Roycroft artisans, Hubbard established a "work and learn", Horace Mann kind of school on the Roycroft Campus. Raymond Riordon was a qualified educator, brought in to be superintendent. Hearing of it, Dard Hunter, then an Ohio State student, was attracted to the Roycroft. Too advanced for student status, his talents were employed in designing this cover for the school's catalog. Rare, quite collectible and valuable.

Hubbard hosted a dinner honoring author Stephen Crane at Buffalo's Genessee Hotel on December 19, 1895. Copies of this dinner program have brought as much as $100 in the Crane/Roycroft collectors' market. The same artwork was used by Hubbard for the May, 1896 issue of the Roycroft Quarterly *magazine.*

period as a lecturer on womens' rights. A particularly attention-getting one was a 10½″ × 14″ placard announcing her lecture, "The New Woman," at the Saint Francis Hotel's Colonial Ball Room on March 17, 1911. Accompanying the printed matter was a fine and large example of artist Gaspard's pen and ink portraiture in his sketch of Alice.

All of these—and some long-forgotten, but unmistakably Roycroft, mementos of yesteryears—are coming forth today and being bought, sold, or exchanged among Roycroft/Hubbard collectors. The search is on-going, exciting, and rewarding in many ways.

Even the hobbies of certain former Roycrofters have produced prized collector pieces. Bertha Hubbard, Elbert's first wife, hand-painted pieces of china and signed them "Hubbard" or "B. C.

Hubbard" at various times from 1894 until at least 1911. She also dated them. Clara Schlagel, a Roycroft book illuminator, had the same hobby and signed her pieces "C.S." Examples of the work of both are in private collections. The art was good and pieces are scarce—and expensive in today's collector market.

3

The Roycroft under Elbert Hubbard II 1915–1938

The leadership of the Roycrofters fell suddenly upon the shoulders of his eldest son when Elbert Hubbard and his wife, Alice, perished in the sinking of the S.S. *Lusitania* by a German U-boat off the coast of Ireland on May 7, 1915.

Elbert Hubbard II had always been close to his father and, though he was first to admit that "there was only one Elbert Hubbard," he was the logical one to take over the helm of an organization that had been uniquely centered about one colorful man for twenty-one years.

Elbert Hubbard had written, impressed, and prospered in an era when Americans mostly stayed at home, read much, and treasured fine home libraries lined with handsomely bound books. This had been undergoing steady change, and Hubbard had certainly been keeping up with the trends—even influencing many of them through his lectures and periodicals.

But Bert Hubbard assumed leadership at a time when a fairly rapid series of marked changes in the American Way of Life were due to occur. By then, talk of a spreading world war and possible United States involvement in it held the attention of everyone.

There followed, in quick succession, this country's involvement in World War I and the eras of the fast automobile, aviation, and radio. All tended to erode the interest of Americans in fine books

As strikingly handsome as his famous father, Elbert Hubbard II looked like this when he assumed the helm of the Roycroft upon the sudden death of Elbert Hubbard in 1915.

and philosophical magazines of the nature that had built the Roycroft. Also, war-born new expertise in mass production methods soon made serious inroads on the markets for the hand-made wares of the Roycroft shops.

But Elbert Hubbard II had enough of his father's magnetic personality and imagination, the loyalty of the Roycrofters, and the lingering, influential memory of his father everywhere, to keep the enterprise afloat for another twenty-three years.

Roycroft Books

Many of the books from the Roycroft Print Shop after Elbert Hubbard II took over the enterprise were reprint, new editions of earlier Roycroft books. But there were also new titles and new authors. During this period also, the Roycrofters printed and bound numerous books for authors on a job basis, similar to what is today referred to as the "vanity" press market. From all indications, the authors of these special issues marketed their own books. Some may have been sold by the Roycroft on a consignment basis. They carried the Roycroft imprint and so there are collectors of these too.

The following is a reasonably complete list of Roycroft issued and sold books of the period covering 1916 through 1937:

Little Journeys to the Homes of the Great (14 vols.)	Hubbard	1916
The Man of Sorrows	Hubbard	1916
Love Poems	Moore	1916
The Romance of Business	Hubbard	1918
In the Spotlight	Hubbard	1918
A Roycroft Anthology	(Various poets)	1918
One Day	Hubbard	1918
I Don't Know, Do You?	Ricker	1918
I'm Not Afraid, Are You?	Ricker	1919
The Liberators	Hubbard	1919
Abe Lincoln and Nancy Hanks	Hubbard	1921
Droll Stories (3 vols.)	Hubbard	1921
The Olympians	Hubbard	1921
Time and Chance	Hubbard	1921
Book of the Roycrofters	Hubbard	1921
Impressions	Hubbard, II	1922
Loyalty in Business	Hubbard	1922
Dreams and Their Meaning	Freud, Dickens, etc.	1922
A Christmas Carol	Dickens	1922
An American Bible	Hubbard, others	1922

The Rubaiyat of Omar Khayyam	Fitzgerald	1922
The Titanic	Hubbard	1923
Where Love Is	Hubbard	1923
The Silver Arrow	Hubbard	1923
Friendship, Love and Marriage (combined with Hubbard's *Little Journey to Thoreau*)	Thoreau, Hubbard	1923
Liberty of Man, Woman and Child	Ingersoll	1924
Roycroft Birthday Book	Hubbard	1924
Poor Richard's Almanac	Franklin	1924
Notebook of Elbert Hubbard	Hubbard	1926
Message to Garcia (MSS reproduction)	Hubbard	1926
Life of Ali Baba	Hubbard	1926
Elbert Hubbard of East Aurora	Shay	1926
Rubaiyat of Omar Khayyam	Fitzgerald	1926
Sermon on the Mount	Jesus	1926
Rhymes of Mother Goose (illustrated by McCandlish)		1927
Selected Writings of Hubbard (14 vols)	Hubbard	1928
The Elbert Hubbard I Knew	Heath	1929
Advertising and Advertisements	Hubbard	1929
The Philosophy of Elbert Hubbard	Hubbard	1930
Bumps, The Golf Ball Kid	McMahon	1930
Elbert Hubbard Speaks	Hubbard	1933
Little Journeys to the Elect	Hubbard	1934
No Enemy but Himself	Hubbard	1934
Gospels of Courage	Bowman	1937

Probably the widest circulation of any of the Roycroft-printed books of this period were the fourteen volume sets of Hubbard's, *Little Journeys* (1916) and his *Selected Writings* (1928). The national marketing of these two sets was placed in the hands of William L. Wise & Co. of New York City who made them tremendously popular. It was a wise move on the part of Elbert Hubbard II. A variety of Roycroft bindings, from buckram to leatherette, to modeled leather was available to the purchasers. In addition, in the better bindings, a "specially prepared for" page was tipped in with the buyer's name printed thereon. Easily found, in any of the bindings, ten years ago at used book stores for as little as $5 for a complete set, they bring $60 to $100 a set today!

Roycroft Magazines

With the cessation of publication of the *Philistine* magazine in 1915, people were left with one periodical, the *FRA*.

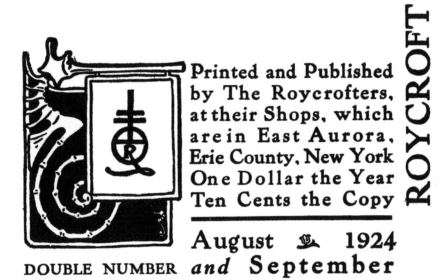

Roycroft

Prove your worth by work

Printed and Published
by The Roycrofters,
at their Shops, which
are in East Aurora,
Erie County, New York
One Dollar the Year
Ten Cents the Copy

August **1924**
DOUBLE NUMBER *and* **September**

The Roycroft magazine was the successor to the Fra *which ended with the August 1917 issue. Vol. 1, No. 1 of the Roycroft was the September 1917 issue.*

A talented writer, Edward J. (Felix) Shay, the magazine's business manager under Elbert Hubbard, creator and original editor, was named editor by Elbert Hubbard II after Hubbard's death. John T. Hoyle was named managing editor. Elbert Hubbard II did by-line commentary.

The *FRA* continued in publication until August, 1917 (vol. 19 no. 5) and was abandoned in favor of a smaller (5″ × 7″), more economical to print periodical, *The Roycroft.* Possibly partly for economy and partly to remind readers of the good old days of Elbert Hubbard and his original *Philistine,* the familiar butcher paper cover reappeared. Volume 1, number 1 of the *Roycroft* made its debut in September, 1917. Elbert Hubbard II became the editor-in-chief.

114

The Grip & Word

Being a Handclasp and Howdy of
The Roycrofters

| Vol. I | MARCH 1922 | No. 1 |

ELBERT HUBBARD, Founder of The Roycrofters
Born at Bloomington, Illinois, June 18, 1859   Lost on the Lusitania May 7, 1915

Collectors finding a copy of The Grip & Word *will have a rare acquisition. It was a 1922 experiment of Elbert Hubbard II to test appeal for a new magazine. It didn't survive beyond the Vol. 1, No. 1, shown here. Black printing on a white cover stock,* it was 4½" x 6½" in size.

The Roycroft magazine lasted until March, 1926, the last issue being volume 17, no. 6. After a two months hiatus that saw the organization without any periodical for the first time since 1895, Elbert Hubbard II came forth in June, 1926 with the *Roycrofter*. It was slightly larger (6″ × 9″) but continued the butcher paper covers. It was to be issued every other month, a further sign of the waning fortunes of the Roycroft enterprises. This effort was abandoned with the September, 1932 issue.

In 1935, the final effort came with a publication that was little more than a pamphlet. It contained only a few pages, was 3″ × 5″ in size, and was issued on no apparent schedule. It was called *Elbert Hubbard's Magazine*. The end came after five issues.

Vol. 4   **November 1929**   **No. 3**

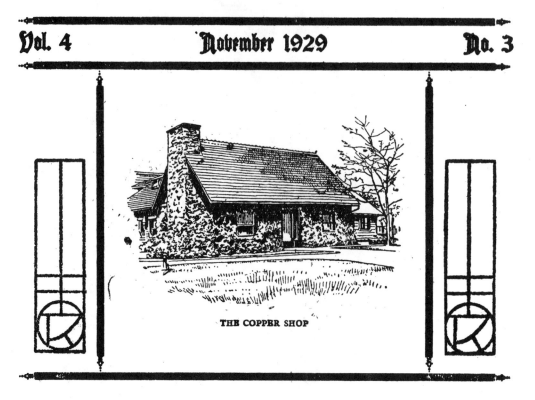

THE COPPER SHOP

A Magazine Devoted to Roycroft Ideals

Printed and Published every little while by

The Roycrofters at their Shops which are in East Aurora, Erie County, State of New York

❧

Subscription Price: One Dollar

The Roycrofter *magazine succeeded the* Roycroft *magazine. Its first issue was June 1926. The March 1926 issue was the last one under the earlier title of* Roycroft. *There was a two-months lapse of publications in the change over.*

The final publication from the Roycroft press was Elbert Hubbard's Monthly *magazine. It followed the demise of the* Roycrofter *magazine in 1932 . . . but not until 1935 . . . and it lasted only a few months. There were but seven issues to collect. Indications are that the circulation was minimal. Rare and important as a "decline of the movement" item. Title was printed over a green background solid circle, printed on bright orange cover stock.*

The *Roycroft* and *Roycrofter* magazines frequently carried illustrated advertisements for Roycroft products through the years. Collectors regard them as the next best thing to Roycroft catalogs for guides as to what to look for. As a consequence, such issues bring almost as much as the catalogs. All have value as reference material on the history of the Roycroft and, as such, are much collected. The same is true of the *FRA*.

For instance, the June, 1916 issue of the *FRA* carried illustrated ads for Roycroft copper and leather goods. In it also were four pages of photos of Roycroft employees, a preview of the twenty-first Annual Convention of the Philistines and an ad announcing a Roycroft Outdoor Summer School of Art to be conducted by artists Fournier and Landeau. And, to the delight to today's antique car buffs, the issue contains informative and illustrative ads on the Detroit, Chalmers, Saxon, and others.

Roycroft Artists and Craftsmen

Aside from the previously mentioned artists, craftsmen, and other personalities who continued to work for different lengths of time at the Roycroft after Elbert Hubbard II assumed leadership of the organization, few became widely known. But the Roycroft continued to attract and/or develop many persons of exceptional talent. The quality of Roycroft books and wares remained high to the very end.

Much of what was produced consisted of new versions of the earlier, time-tested items of proven customer appeal, but some new talent and products did come out of this later period. One was an expert woodcarver and his works were offered for sale by the Roycrofters.

Charles S. Hall came to the organization in 1928 at the age of fifty. By the end of the following year he was the subject of a feature article in the conservative *Buffalo Evening News* which referred to him as being "world famous." Certainly, to the extent that some of the Roycroft visitors from all over the world brought and proudly carried away his carved pieces, this was so. From small plaques, to decorative screens to beautifully carved chests, his one-man output was quickly snapped up.

A native of Prattsburg, New York, Hall had been kidnapped at the age of seven and had never afterwards been reunited with his natural parents. He took up wood carving, he said, during his formative years under the roof of the couple who had kidnapped him. He carved then with a penknife in his lonely attic room and told the reporter that he still used a penknife" in 70 percent of his work" at the Roycroft. Whatever, the things he made at the Roycroft from 1928 until its doors closed in 1938, were indisputably exceptional examples of the art. Some few examples are known to be in private collections today. Their value would be difficult to estimate. There are no known reports of recent sales of any examples of his work.

The July, 1930, *Roycrofter* magazine does provide a clue as to what they could be worth today. A tall, four-panel room screen, carved in oak by Hall to frame a sectional lake scene painted in oil on canvas by a Richard Krueger, was offered at $800. Individuals could commission Hall, through the Roycroft, to decoratively carve their own pieces for anywhere from $85 to $300. As their ad put it:

> We will carve any sort of Old Wooden Box for you and make it into a Hope Chest, a Linen Chest, or a Treasure Chest, and we will do the work as well as we know how. . . . No copies but all in original designs.

Ad in the Roycrofter *magazine gives evidence that wood carver, Charles S. Hall, the last prominent furniture artisan of the Roycroft, turned out expensive pieces. They are not easy to spot and validate as "Roycroft" today.*

Doors Close: The End of An Era

The stock market crash of 1929 caught an entire nation off guard. Elbert Hubbard II and the Roycrofters were no exception. They had been incorporated back in the early 1900s. The stock had always been closely held. Most of it was within the Hubbard family,

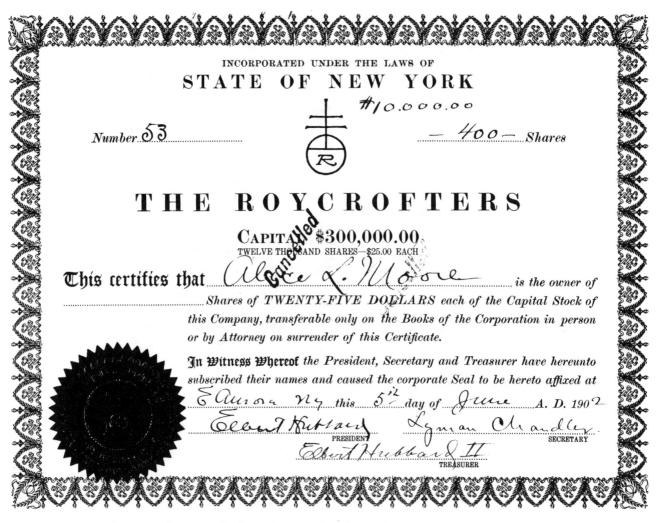

INCORPORATED UNDER THE LAWS OF

STATE OF NEW YORK

#10.000.00

Number 53

— 400 — Shares

THE ROYCROFTERS

CAPITAL $300,000.00

TWELVE THOUSAND SHARES—$25.00 EACH

This certifies that *Alice L. Moore* is the owner of

.... Shares of TWENTY-FIVE DOLLARS each of the Capital Stock of this Company, transferable only on the Books of the Corporation in person or by Attorney on surrender of this Certificate.

In Witness Whereof the President, Secretary and Treasurer have hereunto subscribed their names and caused the corporate Seal to be hereto affixed at

Aurora N.Y. this *5th* day of *June* A. D. 190*2*

Elbert Hubbard
PRESIDENT

Lyman Chandler
SECRETARY

Elbert Hubbard II
TREASURER

The Roycrofters went bankrupt in 1938 but their old stock certificates are among items collected by today's Roycroft buffs.

though some of the employees held a few shares each. And, from time-to-time "Bert" had offered a few shares of 7 percent preferred stock to the public through his magazine. Fortunately, however, the stock had not been so widely dispersed as to make it possible for anyone to pick up a controlling interest for a few cents on the dollar as did occur with some firms at that time. (The old stock certificates are collectors' items today.)

The organization remained intact but problems were mounting and soon began to affect the operations. Roycroft products, as relatively moderate in price as they were, soon represented something of an unneeded luxury to a large segment of the buying public. The Roycroft Inn which "Bert" and his wife, Alta, had built into a popular vacation site, soon experienced a dropping off in patronage. The department stores across the nation, feeling the same pinch, cut back on their orders of Roycroft products for resale.

Gradually it became necessary for Bert to cut back expenses to a place where they would be more in line with income. Production was curtailed and the workforce reduced. Even the lone salesman who had been on the road calling on department stores had to be let go. The taking of these steps delayed the inevitable until 1938 by which time the bare-bone fixed expenses, plus outstanding obligations which would have been in line under a normal economy, combined to force placing the enterprise into receivership.

Elbert Hubbard II had successfully guided the enterprise for twenty-three years after his father's death—three years longer than the father had—but an era had ended. It had been an exciting one that had given new impetus and direction to the Arts & Crafts in America.

So indelible was the mark, that it was inevitable that one day there would be a revived interest in Elbert Hubbard and his Roycrofters.

4

Afterglow and Lingering Interest 1938–2000

The Receivers in Bankruptcy were soon flooded with individuals and organizations seeking to take over the entire complex with its many buildings spread over a "campus" that dominated both sides of East Aurora's Grove Street for a full block and beyond. Several were given the opportunity to try but, in fairness to them, if the Hubbard mystique and Elbert Hubbard II's considerable management skills had not been able to turn the trick, no one could have then duplicated a crafts complex that had been uniquely centered around one man. So they failed.

One by one the Roycroft buildings were sold and put to new uses. Fortunately, none of the new owners of the various buildings (nor their successive owners over the years) made any substantial changes in their exteriors. Overall, the Roycroft Campus looks much the same today as it did when it cradled and nourished a Morris-like, new-to-America, adventure in Arts and Crafts.

A man unusually devoted to his father, Elbert Hubbard II did much to keep alive the public interest in Hubbard and the Roycrofters after 1938. From then forward to the time of his own death in 1970, he corresponded with Hubbard devotees and students all over the world. He lectured and wrote articles, gave interviews, and engaged in the business of buying and selling out-of-print Roycroft books. His daughter and granddaughter pursued the same business after his death.

There had been three biographies of Elbert Hubbard published between 1901 and 1929 and one in 1940. Thereafter 23 years passed

122

Elbert Hubbard II in 1938, the year that saw the Roycroft enterprises finally fall victim to the depression that followed the stock market crash of 1929.

In the
District Court of the United States
for the Western District of New York.

In the Matter of the Petition

of

THE ROYCROFTERS, Debtor

For Relief Under Section 77-B of the
Bankruptcy Act as Amended

Proceedings for the
Reorganization of
the Corporation

No. 27358

PLAN OF REORGANIZATION

OF

THE ROYCROFTERS

Dated as of July 20, 1938

The estimates, statements, explanations and suggestions contained in this Plan of Reorganization and in any note, circular or communication issued, or which may hereafter be issued with relation thereto are for the guidance of the Court and of the creditors of the Roycrofters and are not intended to be, are not to be accepted or relied upon by any creditor of the Roycrofters or by any other person as a warranty for any purpose with respect to this Plan of Reorganization. No one is authorized to make any statements regarding this Plan of Reorganization, which are not set forth herein.

Immediately following the bankruptcy of the Roycrofters in 1938, attempts were made to revive it. Such efforts were to no avail even though the receivers came up with a plan and the community was urged, through newspaper ads to get behind the effort. Samuel R. Guard, a newcomer to East Aurora, was first to try, but the attempt (mostly directed toward commercial printing) was short-lived.

Elbert Hubbard II in his eighties, posed before an East Aurora Main St. landmark—the huge Jerome Conner bronze statue of his father unveiled in 1930. The Roycroft's first and only sculptor came back, after many years absence, came back for the unveiling of the work the Roycrofters had commissioned him to do when the organizations end seemed to be in sight. Photo courtesy of Rile Prosser, Photo-journalist

before another book apeared; that, in 1963. A small book, *Little Journeys to The Homes of Roycrofters* contained brief biographies of both Elbert Hubbard and Elbert Hubbard II and a number of Roycrofters. Since the early 1960s there has been a continuing upsurge in local interest and an ever-widening interest nationwide and beyond. An Elbert Hubbard Library-Museum was founded in 1962 and is now located on Oakwood Avenue in the village, housed in a 1910 craftsman-style bungalow that had been the home and studio of George ScheideMantel, a Roycroft master craftsman and one-time head of the Roycroft leather shop.

In 1976, the Roycrofters-At-Large-Association was organized to help spread word of a Roycroft Renaissance. It now enjoys a nationwide membership and conducts an annual arts and crafts festival.

The Roycroft Campus—consisting of 14 buildings—became a National Historic Landmark in 1986 and the momentum in the spread of renewed interest widened considerably. Exhibits of Roycroft crafts were held in the Buffalo area and northern Pennsylvania.

In October 1994 the Memorial Art Gallery of the University of Rochester opened an impressive exhibition, "Head, Heart and Hand: Elbert Hubbard and the Roycrofters" that traveled on a national coast-to-coast tour, ending in 1996. The exhibition's 168-page catalog with color illustrations is filled with Roycroft history.

Across the tree-lined street from the Roycroft Inn, a brick-paved "Appian Way" path through the center of the Roycroft Campus was restored and opened in 1999 by the Roycrofters-At-Large-Association after a successful fund drive.

The Roycroft Inn, beautifully restored, reopened in June of 1995, having been closed during an eight-million-dollar restoration. Today, guests arrive from all around the nation and abroad to enjoy the unique atmosphere of the Roycroft Campus as they did at the turn of the last century.

5

More Collectibles and the Roycroft Renaissance

Elbert Hubbard's Roycroft complex was more than just a shop for the handcrafting of leather, brass, copper, silver items, a Mission-style furniture manufacturing shop, a print shop, sculptors' and artists' studios, bank, inn and gift shop. Uniquely it was all rolled into one. There was simply nothing quite like it in the United States back then. And nothing quite like it since.

Small wonder then, that it beckoned the curious, the vacationing and the inspired from all walks of life. Making the trek to East Aurora were many of the greats and near greats of the time, as well as those aspiring to greatness or mere satisfaction in their chosen fields of art, literature or craftsmanship.

Collectors Seek Filled Roycroft Autograph Books

The Roycrofters "can do" spirit exerted a lasting magnetism. It also bequeathed a vast legacy of collectors' items of exceptional value.

As noted earlier, there is considerable interest today in the sketches and paintings of Roycroft artists and designers. Particularly is this true of the works of Dard Hunter, Alexis Fournier, W. W. Denslow, Burt Barnes, Jules Gaspard, Otto Schneider, Sammy Warner, Raymond Nott, and Albert Miller. The interest now goes beyond their major works

Roycroft autograph/guest book, limp leather cover, with lettering in gold.

(which keep growing in value) to practically any signed piece they might have turned out in impromptu fashion for a friend or admirer.

As always, there is great and continuing interest, too, in collecting letters and signatures of famous persons of by-gone days. Only a few Roycrofters, other than Elbert and Alice Hubbard, attained sufficient fame in their day as to make their signatures alone worth money today. Some exceptions would be Dard Hunter, Fournier, and Denslow.

However, because many famous persons came to the Roycroft as guests or convention speakers, thousands of visitors and Roycrofters of lesser fame sought them out to sign limp-leather autograph books, purchased, of course, at the Roycroft Gift Shop. Often, Roycroft employees and other East Aurorans would persuade famous persons to write a few words above their signatures or draw a sketch. Naturally, these autograph-seekers took their books back home to treasure and save.

So, today, as attics and trunks are emptied most anywhere in the U.S. or Canada, these sometimes seemingly worthless old books are trashed or sold for a pittance in a yard sale. This is often so because not all of the Roycroft-made signature books bear the now-familiar identifying trademark. Some have it at the lower right of the front cover, but others that do not can be spotted only if one is familiar with the traditional limp-leather cover with "Roycroftie" lettering in gold and sometimes tooling bordering the title. These characteristics signal to collectors that valuable signatures could well be on the pages within the aging and often deteriorating covers.

What is particularly interesting about many of the signatures is that the famous signers were so caught up with the Roycroft spirit of camaraderie that, in pen and ink, they waxed eloquent, poetic, and artistic, and didn't just jot down their signatures. That often makes their signatures more valuable today.

Aside from these once truly famous persons, it is important for collectors to know that certain of the Roycrofters who were asked to place their autographs in the books, back when they were of importance only at the Roycroft Campus, have risen to genuine fame in the Arts and Crafts movement. In recent years, interest in the Arts and Crafts has moved front and center in histories and exhibitions focusing upon America's cultural emergence and advancement.

From this author's collection of Roycroft autograph/guest books, presented here are some examples of what you, also, might expect to find most anywhere, if you remain on the alert.

Clockwise from top left: (1) After leaving Roycroft, artist W. W. Denslow became famous as the illustrator of L. Frank Baum's The Wizard of Oz. *(2) Watercolor by Roycroft artist Raymond Nott for an employee who worked in the dining room of The Roycroft Inn (3) Roycroft artist Jules Gaspard was not particularly famous in his day, but now his art is becoming collectible. (4) One-time head of the Roycroft art department, Alexis Fournier gained independent fame for his oil paintings.*

Dard Hunter, one-time artist/designer at the Roycroft, went on to lasting fame as the world's foremost authority on paper-making. His art, on whatever it is found, generally doubles its collector value.

Broadening Interest

As evidenced by prices noted in this edition, the market for all things Roycroft and Roycroft-related has dramatically increased from 1980 when the first edition of Roycroft Collectibles was published. But beyond the books, leather, furniture and art metal, collectors now seek and pay handsomely for photgraphs, art, sketches, convention programs, catalogs, letterheads and letters, brochures, pins, buttons, and other ephemera. once regarded as worthless.

And in recent years, interest has increased in collecting the works and related memorabilia of early Roycrofters who left the campus to strike

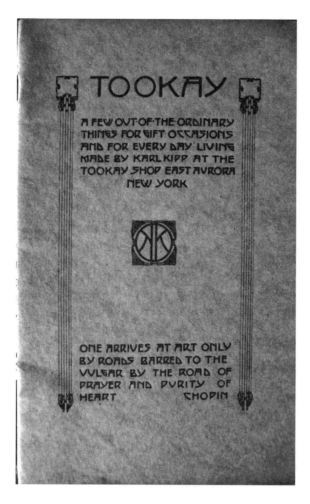

TOOKAY

A FEW OUT-OF-THE-ORDINARY
THINGS FOR GIFT OCCASIONS
AND FOR EVERY DAY LIVING
MADE BY KARL KIPP AT THE
TOOKAY SHOP EAST AURORA
NEW YORK

ONE ARRIVES AT ART ONLY
BY ROADS BARRED TO THE
VULGAR BY THE ROAD OF
PRAYER AND PURITY OF
HEART   CHOPIN

Wise collectors are always on the lookout for variant copies of Karl Kipp's catalogs, because they picture his pieces, give dimensions, and are invaluable in the search for Kipp originals.

out on their own, continuing their work in their own shops, under their own trademarks.

This has become particularly so in the case of Karl Kipp who headed the Roycroft copper shop before founding his own Tookay Shop. Items with Kipp's Tookay Shop trademark have, in recent years, sold at figures even exceding the prices for Roycroft pieces.

Karl Kipp's Tookay mark.

Kipp issued a number of catalogs which pictured and described his pieces in colorful, persuasive prose and, where space permitted, he would add a bit of original or borrowed philosophy. His description of one of his bud vases read:

"One rose is enough if it is a beautiful one and if it has a lovely setting. This unique vase is of hand-hammered copper and fitted with a glass

Poet, playwright, author of books on Japanese art, Sadakichi Hartmann was a writer-in-residence at the Roycroft for a time. In the 1970s, the University of California, Riverside, published the quarterly Sadakichi Hartmann Newsletter, *designed to stimulate research and gather his scattered materials and writings. Hartmann died in 1944. This was his contribution to a fan's autograph book at the Roycroft in 1909.*

flower holder designed for a single blossom. It has grace and symmetry and will give a touch of simplicity and loveliness to any room. It is 8" high and the price is $1.00"

But Kipp didn't stop there with his sentimental, philosophical sell. Beside the photograph illustrating the vase with a rose in place, he included this penetrating thought, placed within quotation marks indicating that it was a verity familiar to all: "Walls crumble and rotting empires fall. The rotting nations drop from off Time's bough, and only the things that the dreamers make live on."

New Collectibles Result of Roycroft Renaissance

As noted earlier in this book, a small group of Hubbard/Roycroft afficianados formed the Roycrofters-At-Large Association in 1976.

A revival of the Roycroft craftsmanship is now going strong in East Aurora. A new generation of artisans, creating under the banner of the Roycrofters-at-Large have adopted this trademakr, the double Rs standing for Roycroft Renaissance.

They were bent upon bringing about a revival of the Hubbard/Roycroft spirit of "Hand, Heart, and Brain" in cultural ways, including the creation of worthy Arts and Crafts items to rival those of the original Roycrofters.

Among the founders was the late Rix Jennings, son of Walter U. Jennings, an early and superb coppersmith whose Roycroft work (and personal output from his own shop after the Roycroft shops closed) are now sought-after collectibles. Rix, himself a noted artist whose work includes a number of beautiful watercolors of the Roycroft Campus, was called upon to design the RALA trademark. He incorporated a second letter R to call attention to the renaissance of the Roycroft movement, while retaining the distinguishing features of the original mark to remind new craftsmen of the heritage handed down by the

Internationally known poet Richard LeGallienne spent two summers at the Roycroft Campus. He penned this poem in a fan's Roycroft autograph book when there in 1908.

The Roycroft Campus in East Aurora, New York. consists of nine buildings on the National Register of Historic Places. It is interesting to visit not only for its historical significance but also to see the work of today's Roycroft artisans.

original Roycrofters. The cross arms were slightly altered, the left side pointing down to signify the early roots with Elbert Hubbard's Roycroft, with the right side pointing up to indicate future growth and progress.

The right to use the new mark is zealously guarded and jury-granted only to those whose works measure up to carefully drawn standards. The results today are distinctive objets d' art created by independent artisans on (and sometimes off) the Roycroft Campus and bearing the new mark.

These are likely to become tomorrow's Roycroft collectibles even as they have become almost instant ones today. This, because of their present and enduring attractiveness. Moreover, not being mass-produced, their relative current and ultimate scarcity attracts collectors.

Varied artisans have now been producing items (furniture, pottery, jewelry, paintings, graphics, stained glass, weavings, etc.) for 20 years, and already there are collectors seeking "early Roycroft Renaissance" pieces while adding current ones to their collections. There well may emerge from among the new Roycrofters, some who will be accorded late-arriving fame over and above the already recognized talent of the group. Their present work, already highly collectible, could well become even more prized decades from now. Such is the history of the Arts and Crafts movement. Most certainly, as a group, they will all have a place in the growing Roycroft niche in the Arts and Crafts movement in America.

The Roycrofters-At-Large-Association's online newsletter and home page is hosted by The Webpage of The Roycrofters (www.roycrofter.com). There, can be found information about the artisans as well as the various activities it sponsors in addition to the annual Roycroft Summer Festival.

6
Searching for Roycroft
In the Second Millenium

For all of its shortcomings in terms of the thrill of the hunt, the information super highway wins hands-down over literal highways and back roads in terms of cold, impersonal efficiency. The quest for that long-elusive Roycroft item of one's dreams may now be only a mouse-click or two away, and the cost of fulfilling the dream—well, judge for yourself! Every price noted in this chapter was gleaned online from live auction results, galleries, Internet auctions, and antiquarian book search engines. We anticipate such trends and pricing throughout the year 2001 and beyond. We've mixed a little history and perspective in this chapter along with the current prices—and you'll find some interesting earlier price history in the preceding chapters.

Early Books

Considering the fact that total press runs of most early Roycroft titles were counted in mere hundreds, it's a tribute to their initial worthiness that so many survived—and fascinating to find where they've popped up for sale in the nation and the world. At live auctions, on antiquarian booksellers' Internet search engines and online auctions, we were able to locate 88 of 104 Roycroft books (see pages 26-28) published between 1896 and 1915.

One certainty is that there will be no more copies than there are now. But, due largely to online auctions and search engines, prices for some titles vary to extremes both well above and below what collectors and dealers may have considered "the norm" just a few years ago. As a lengthy June 18, 1999 *Wall Street Journal* article entitled "Untidy Shelves: The Internet Shakes Up Rare Books" pointed out, "The Internet is radically transforming the rare book market.

"Simply put, many rare books aren't rare any more. People who would search for years for a book now find it with the click of a mouse. As a result, prices for 20th century books are falling through the floor, along with the value of some collectors' libraries... But the volume of business and the number of 'rare' book collectors jumping into the hobby is exploding, as are prices for the truly scarce books."

"Truly scarce" applies to numbers of first-edition Roycroft books, and especially to the very limited variant editions of the same titles with special bindings, papers, hand-illumination or significant provenance. Take, for instance, the 1901 Roycroft printing of Robert Louis Stevenson's *Will O' The Mill*. Number one of 100 numbered copies bound in three quarter leather, printed on Japan vellum, signed by Elbert Hubbard and the illuminator, and inscribed by its original owner who was Hubbard's sister-in-law, was offered on The Webpage of The Roycrofters in December 1998 for $900. We located several other copies at varying prices. A good copy of an edition limited to 350 copies, bound in suede and signed by Hubbard and the illuminator, brought $61 in an online auction in September 2000. Bottom end of the range? A copy of the regular edition with its suede cover "very worn and discolored, but very good text," offered by a dealer on the Advanced Book Exchange for $20!

While this is an extreme example, and while each of the price extremes could well represent a good value for the prospective owners' individual purposes, the volatility caused by Internet listings and auctions can still translate to opportunity for the savvy collector or savvy dealer—whichever is first—to spot that occasional "steal." For instance, not a single bookseller among all of those listed on Advanced Book Exchange, Bibliocity or Bibliofind could offer a copy of *Song of Songs*, the first Roycroft Book (pages 19-20) at any price. This 1896 book turned up on eBay and sold for a mere $360. Expect buys like these which aren't first grabbed by caring collectors for their treasured libraries to find their ways back to dealers' shelves—at a substantial mark-up! (We were right! A later check before sending this manuscript turned up a copy for $575.)

Any 19th century Roycroft title is a collectible by virtue of age and scarcity, but some have special appeal because of their colorful origins or notable contemporary authors. One such book, pictured on page 5 of the color plate and offered by an online bookseller for $1000 is the 1898 Roycroft edition of *The Dipsy Chanty* by Rudyard Kipling. Hubbard republished the popular contemporary author's original work without permission and was sued. Most copies were sold before the suit was settled in 1899 for a $75 fee to Kipling's attorney and return of the remaining books. In this writer's collection of correspondence between Hubbard and the attorney, the attorney asked Hubbard for copies of the leather-bound edition of *A Message to Garcia*, which was advertised in Hubbard's popular *Philistine* magazine. In a following letter acknowledging receipt of remaining copies of *The Dipsy Chanty*, the attorney wrote, "Please accept my thanks for the copies of your leather bound Garcias—they are very handsome—I shall send one to Mr. Kipling."

George Bernard Shaw didn't fare as well from a legal standpoint when Hubbard edited and published Shaw's essay *On Going to Church* in 1896. For more about this, and the variant editions of the 40-page publication, see pages 24-25. Of the dozen copies offered on bookseller Internet sites, five were between $50 and $80, four between $100 and $185, and three $200-225.

No colorful circumstances surrounded the 1899 Roycroft publication of *Persian Pearl*, so the asking prices of $2000 and $900 for the two copies offered on Internet bookseller listings are likely attributable to the name of the author, colorful and controversial attorney of the era, Clarence Darrow.

Cornerstones of a Hubbard-centered Roycroft collection might include first edition copies of his famous 1899 motivational essay, *A Message to Garcia*, one of which is pictured on page 29, a collection of his "Little Journeys" (see pages 34-35) and a set of *The Complete Writings of Elbert Hubbard*.

We located five copies of the 1899 editions of *A Message to Garcia*, two with paper covers at $10 and $50, three of the limited edition with suede covers at $185 to $450. If you're lucky enough to look through some unsorted old materials, look carefully—none of the editions exceeded 14 pages. *Little Journeys* took forms from the original pamphlet-style versions sold by subscription, to large individual volumes and compilations and complete sets. These were produced in great numbers, so their value lies as much in their content as in their collectibility. Individual *Little Journeys* may be found on eBay and in used book stores as well as antiquarian booksellers for as little as $5, though some large volumes, particularly if signed and numbered, bring prices similar to other Roycroft books. Those interested in reading a complete matched set may want to check for ones later published by Wm. Wise & Co., New York.

The 1000 sets of *The Complete Writings of Elbert Hubbard* were issued beginning in 1908 and periodically through completion in 1915. Unless they were later rebound, you'll not find a set where the leather color of the 20 large volumes matches throughout. Our Internet search of online booksellers yielded nine complete sets at prices ranging from a low of $2950 up to $5500, with the rest between $3000 and $4000. Single volumes or groups of several are sometimes seen, usually within a pro-rated price range equivalent to complete sets, so a patient collector could possibly still gather all twenty.

Catalogs and Magazines

Hubbard's delightful writing style and the sometimes novel design of these pieces makes some Roycroft catalogs treasures in their own right—but as key references to the range of offerings, early catalogs sometimes cost more than the current prices of the items they depicted! Of particular value to bibliophiles are catalogs published between 1900 and 1912.

Like the books themselves, there are also variant editions of the catalogs. Knowing how variant can save researchers a few dollars. For example, this writer's copies of the 1900 edition of *The Book of the Roycrofters* is almost—but not quite—identical to *The Roycroft Books: A Catalog and Some Comments* except for the cover title. Both are gold stamped, suede bound, silk lined, and advertise the same books. The use of a second color and choice of full-page pictures of the shops, campus and workers vary. We saw one copy of the latter version sold on eBay for $53, and several copies of both versions listed by online booksellers at $100 to $150. *The Book of the Roycrofters* appeared again in 1907, this time in boards with a cloth spine. We located two copies, one at $40, the other at $175. The 1908 Christmas catalog with *The Book of the Roycrofters* cover, sold at auction for $114.

Paper-bound *Some Books for Sale at Our Shop* catalogs were issued during the early years. Dealers listed prices averaging around $50 for those issued annually between 1901 and 1904, and we found one listed on eBay at $15. Our Internet search turned up one copy of the 1905-6 *A Catalog of Some Books & Things made by the Roycrofters at their Shop opposite the School House in East Aurora*, offered at $125. In late 2000, copies sold on online auctions for between $22 and $62

Like *The Book of the Roycrofters*, what the cover page says isn't what the title page says! Internet searchers may also want to try *A Catalog of Roycroft Books and Things Year Ten*. The title page—and the rest of the title—is shown on page 25. This paper-bound catalog also includes photos of the campus, lists *Little Journeys* pamphlets for sale, and advertises availability of leather, mattresses, furniture and rag rugs. We found no copies of the 1907-8 catalog. The three-color, paper-bound 1909 *The Roycroft Catalog* (we found one listed at $120) has excellent illustrations of special bindings and offers earlier titles with some of those special bindings at prices up to $250.

The 1910 catalog is done in boards with a cloth spine. Its cover has a raised rendering of the Roycroft Shop, beneath which are raised letters, "Roycroft Shop." Its 128 pages index and illustrate books, copper, leather and mottos. "Roycroft Catalogue" on the cover—and "The Roycroft Catalog 1912, Books, Leather, Copper" on the title page—is 52 pages paper-bound, with more than half illustrating copper and leather. We found neither listed during periodic Internet searches.

Hubbard's two popular magazines, *The Philistine* (see page 32) and *The Fra* (see page 37) provide entertaining insights to both Hubbard and the era. *The Philistine*, in particular, is also a good source of advertisements and information about the various offerings of the Roycroft Shops. We've seen bound volumes (six issues) of *Philistines* listed by Internet booksellers at prices ranging from $20 to $50. eBay is also a good place to look for these. We've seen them listed there with no takers, so an e-mail might land you a set at a bargain price. In September 2000, single issues sold for as low as fifty cents all the way up to $16! A set of 41 bound volumes of *The Philistine* (six issues per volume) went for $250.

Two especially collectible issues are March, 1899, which contained the first and then-untitled printing of "A Message to Garcia," and the June and July 1895 issues which are in the bound Volume No. 1 containing early poetic works of Stephen Crane, author of *The Red Badge of Courage*.

Individual issues of The Fra sell from $10 to $25. A complete run of the magazine went at auction for $1000 in 1999. Volumes of The Fra bound by the Roycrofters are particularly desirable. Six bound volumes, a total of 36 issues from April 1909 through March 1912, sold online for $1225 or $204 per volume in September 2000.

Furniture and Wood Products

The magazine pedestal offered for $20 in an early advertisement pictured on page 44 speaks to the appreciation of Roycroft furniture and decorative wood items. One like it cost its new owner $24,200 at auction in 1999.

Based on auction prices realized in 2000, one could have put together the very beginnings of a cozy Roycroft den for between $17,000 and $44,000 depending on the choice of pieces. A modest one could have included one of the less costly magazine stands (either $8250 or $9350), a 28" wide library table ($4400), a pair of ladder-back chairs ($1320), a rocker ($1760) and a tabouret ($1540) to put beside it. Or, with a bit more room and budget, one could have kept the magazine pedestal, replaced the small library table with one almost five feet wide ($9900), traded the straight chairs for a matched armchair and rocker set ($4400) and a different tabouret ($5225). Nice touches for either would have been a mahogany writing table and desk chair, together $7000.

Large Roycroft pieces generally command five-figure prices at auctions or galleries. We viewed a Roycroft dresser offered at a Manhattan gallery for $13,750 and noted the auction of another at $14,000 plus the 10% buyers premium. At another auction, a sideboard with leaded glass doors was gaveled down at $13,200 including premium. Smaller pieces such as tea tables, tabourets, footstools and chairs vary according to rarity and condition. For instance, two roughly-similar circular tea tables at different auctions brought $3750 and $4250 plus 10%. The higher priced one had Mackmurdo feet. Two open-sided tabourets brought $1540 and $2310 including premium. The second was slightly larger and had a leather top, while the third and more unusual version, at $5225 including premium, had plank sides with keyhole cutouts.

Various styles of Roycroft chairs, from simple side chairs, arms chairs and rockers to massive Morris-style, range from several hundred to several thousand dollars. A Morris-style chair brought $7500. Basic ladder-back side chairs with leather seats like the previously-mentioned pair are often sold in groups rather than individually. Individual arm chairs and rockers, depending on size, rarity and condition brought prices at 1999 auctions ranging between $1300 and $5500 plus premium. Some of these came from the Grove Park Inn and Resort at Asheville, NC, site of the National Arts & Crafts Conference and Antiques Show held each February. Many of the Inn's original furnishings were built by the Roycroft and numbers of these pieces have come to market recently.

Roycroft frames and mirrors may be found marked or unmarked. See the photos on page 47 to help identify unmarked pieces. At different 1999 auctions, an unmarked 34" × 34" hanging mirror with replaced glass brought $1100 while an unmarked 36" × 50" hanging hall mirror brought $2000, both plus buyers premium. A 17 " × 22" Roycroft frame containing a Roycroft motto brought $450 plus premium. For more about mottos, see pages 78-82 and 103.

Early Roycroft furniture catalogs issued between 1904 and 1912 are the source of model numbers often listed by antiques dealers and auctioneers to identify the various pieces. Most are illustrated with photos, though some use drawings. We found none listed during periodic Internet checks. At auction in 1999, 29 looseleaf catalog pages of furniture, lighting and ironwork sold for $400 plus premium.

Indicative of the value—and range—of Roycroft wood products may be the observation, "Old Things Are Best." Carved in to a 10" × 42" ash motto plank along with the Roycroft orb and cross, it was gaveled down at auction for $6500 plus buyer's premium.

On the lower end of the furniture scale, a Little Journeys bookshelf, designed to hold the 14-volume memorial edition of Hubbard's *Little Journeys*, sold for $555 in late 2000. Another one in better condition brought $895 in an online auction. A set of walnut bookends sold for $366. And a stripped out Roycroft "Goody Box" went for $233.

Leather Goods

A 1909 copy of *The Roycroft Leather Book* catalog listed by an antiquarian bookseller at $225 and another sold on eBay for $55 weren't priced that way because they were considered works of art, the Dard

Hunter-designed cover notwithstanding. It's a 46-page photographic guide with the potential for a good return on investment.

The Roycrofters produced leather goods in scores of styles ranging in size from watch fobs to wastebaskets and, though these may not be your primary Roycroft collecting interest, current prices could make it well worth your while to devote an extra few minutes to check for the orb on, or inside, any antique leather you come across in your travels. It may help fund other acquisitions of your choice!

A 17" diameter tooled leather table mat bearing the Roycroft orb brought $3000 plus 10% buyers premium at auction in 1999. A 15" mat of another design is illustrated on page 57, along with a number of other leather items. Take note of the little leather-covered clock on the same page. Including buyers premium it was gaveled down at $8250. Another leather covered clock is pictured on page six of the color plate. When we made that photo arrangement more than 20 years ago, we didn't give a second thought to obscuring a Roycroft leather table mat with other items!

Roycroft leather accessories such as wallets, handbags, (also see page 48) and small cases for items such as gloves, matches and scissors aren't frequently found, and prices vary with condition. At a recent auction a card case brought $190. A worn full-size leather handbag brought $375, while a 3" x 3 " tooled leather saddle purse in exceptional condition auctioned at more than twice that amount. An 8"x 5" tooled leather picture frame with some stains and missing the stand on the back brought $1300 plus 10% buyers premium, and a 9" x 6 " one in excellent shape brought $1500 plus premium. A set of leather bookends brought $395 in an eBay auction.

Metalware and Lighting

From delicate hat pins (see page 52), two of which together brought more than $1300, to hefty andirons which brought more than $2800 including premium at auction in 1999, Roycrofters produced an array of decorative metalware for the home, sold first by mail order and after 1915 at hundreds of selected retailers (see pages 63-67) nationwide. As a result, prices for common forms of smaller pieces such as bookends, candlesticks, vases and trays, smokers' items and desk accessories are often similar whether at galleries, live auctions, or on eBay where metal items are usually present.

Bookends, of which a few of the many styles and sizes are shown on page 53, sold on eBay at prices ranging from $50 to $450 on periodic checks as recently as October 2000, with most from $100-$200. At a gallery's online listing we found them from $110 to $325, and at live auction from $200 to $500, where a pair like the ones shown on page three of the color plate brought $300 plus premium.

As the advertisement on page 53 illustrates, the Roycrofters made candlesticks "for all purposes" from utilitarian to decorative. Tall candlesticks like the pair on page eight of the color plate brought $534 on eBay, while other tall styles brought $475 to $650 plus premium at live auction. Gallery prices ranged from $225 for a pair of 2" high candlesticks to $975 for a pair of Karl Kipp design Princess candlesticks. A single wall sconce of a different style than the one on page 54 brought $215 on eBay while a pair brought $483, and another pair fetched $600 at live auction. A candle holder like the one shown on page 54 sold for $143.

Roycroft vases came in forms from the bud vase shown on page four of the color plate ($350 plus premium at live auction) to the often-sought "American Beauty" style (page 56, No. c-201), $1500 plus premium for this 19" high model at another auction. American beauty styles were made in varying heights. A damaged 17" version brought $900 plus premium and a 12" one sold on eBay for $1200. A 6" version sold for $1825 in late 2000. At live auctions, most other styles were gaveled down in the $500-$1000 range, though the highest brought $4750 plus premium and the 6" high vase with Steuben glass insert (see page58) brought $210 plus premium.

Simple bowls and trays brought prices in the $350-$899 range, though footed or covered pieces can command four figures. A simple serving tray like the one on page three of the color plate brought $325 on eBay and a 6" diameter bowl like the one on page seven of the color plate and page 55 brought $550 plus premium at auction. A 5" diameter illustrated on page 58 was gallery priced at $395 and another sold online for $214.

Matched desk sets (see pages 55-56) came in several motifs with varied numbers of individual accessories. A seven-piece set including a perpetual calendar with original cards brought $2200 plus premium at auction while a five-piece set sold on eBay for $1200, both in September 1999. Letter openers (see page 54) in various sizes and designs brought between $50 and $100 both on eBay and at live auctions, and other single pieces such as pen trays, letter holders (see page 48) ink wells and blotter corners appear periodically on eBay, generally near $100 and up.

Numerous items for smokers (see page 62) from humidors to ash trays are found at live auctions and on eBay. A cigarette holder (item 638) sold for $125 on eBay while a pair of ashtrays/matchbook holders similar to item 646 brought $100 and an ornate hammered copper humidor brought $1100 plus premium, both at live auction. A five-piece smoking set sold for $511. Elbert Hubbard rarely, if ever, smoked and the Roycroft didn't make cigars—but the cigar box bearing his image, shown on the back cover, attracted $600 plus premium!

A Roycroft lamp of the same style but a different color Steuben glass shaft shown on page six of the color plate auctioned for $600 and the one one page seven of the color plate brought $2000, both plus premium. The lamp pictured on the back cover brought $2600 plus premium. A lamp of a style not illustrated brought $675 on eBay. A boudoir lamp with a leaded glass shade designed by Dard Hunter brought $4750 plus premium at auction, and a gallery listed the lamp pictured on page 59 (number 906) at $3850. Two Roycroft chandeliers brought $4500 and $8500 plus premium at auction.

Other Collectibles

Bringing $350 plus premium at auction, salt and pepper shakers like those on page 109 indicate the interest in original Buffalo Pottery china made for the Roycroft. Other pieces, such as a teapot and sugar bowl (see back cover), together auctioned for $1000 and a footed compote brought $1350, both plus premium. Also made for the Roycroft were "little brown jugs" which have appeared recently in great numbers and other colors and can be found for as little as $10, with other hues bringing more. The best assurance of authenticity, and also costlier and rarer, are ones (see page 72) with the original tassle attached. A later item, a punch bowl and set of eight cups, went for $279 at auction.

This chapter reports some current prices on items pictured throughout the book—but it doesn't say you can't find them for less. You may just need to turn off the computer and get back on the literal highway! Happy hunting!

Index